blue
rider
press

What It Means to Be a Democrat

BLUE RIDER PRESS

a member of

Penguin Group (USA) Inc.

New York

WHAT
IT MEANS
TO BE A
DEMOCRAT

GEORGE MCGOVERN

with Linda Kulman

blue
rider
press

Published by the Penguin Group
Penguin Group (USA) Inc., 375 Hudson Street, New York, New York
10014, USA • Penguin Group (Canada), 90 Eglinton Avenue East, Suite 700, Toronto,
Ontario M4P 2Y3, Canada (a division of Pearson Penguin Canada Inc.) • Penguin Books Ltd,
80 Strand, London WC2R 0RL, England • Penguin Ireland, 25 St Stephen's Green, Dublin 2,
Ireland (a division of Penguin Books Ltd) • Penguin Group (Australia), 250 Camberwell Road,
Camberwell, Victoria 3124, Australia (a division of Pearson Australia Group Pty Ltd) •
Penguin Books India Pvt Ltd, 11 Community Centre, Panchsheel Park, New Delhi–110 017,
India • Penguin Group (NZ), 67 Apollo Drive, Rosedale, North Shore 0632, New Zealand
(a division of Pearson New Zealand Ltd) • Penguin Books (South Africa) (Pty)
Ltd, 24 Sturdee Avenue, Rosebank, Johannesburg 2196, South Africa

Penguin Books Ltd, Registered Offices: 80 Strand, London WC2R 0RL, England

ISBN 978-0-399-15822-3

Printed in the United States of America
1   3   5   7   9   10   8   6   4   2

Book design by Claire Naylon Vaccaro

For Eleanor,
who converted me from Republican
to Democrat.

CONTENTS

What It Means to Be a Democrat

INTRODUCTION

Whenever I hear the phrase "big tent," I'm reminded of the tabernacle at the Holiness Campground. It was on the James River, known locally as the Jim River, four miles east of Mitchell, South Dakota, where I grew up. My minister father led a congregation of Wesleyan Methodists, and my family would go to the tabernacle, with its straw-covered floor, every night for two weeks each summer to take part in the crusades. We were all of the same faith, some of us once-a-year worshippers and others daily churchgoers. We came together to hear the same sermons, but each of us took from these homilies what we needed. Some attendees were "saved" and dropped to their knees in tears at the altar. Others, including me, usually just watched from the back row. I respected the earnestness of the preachers and the worshippers.

The Democratic Party is much the same: millions of people with varying ideas and differing degrees of faith in specific ideals. There are as many definitions of what it means to be a Democrat as there are Democrats.

I am not writing this book to proselytize for politics (and certainly not for religion). Ideologically speaking, anyone who claims to be a Democrat belongs under the same big tent. As Thomas Jefferson, who organized what evolved into the modern Democratic Party, famously said, "I never considered a difference of opinion in politics, in religion, in philosophy, as cause for withdrawing from a friend." I don't detest the Democrats who disagree with me, as many of them did in the 1960s and in my 1972 presidential campaign when I fought with all my strength to bring our boys home from the tragically mistaken American war in Vietnam. Presidents

Kennedy, Johnson, and Vice President Humphrey all supported this war. All of them were strong Democrats whom I admired and considered friends. If I should meet them in the mystery beyond the grave, I'd embrace them—even though they were wrong about Vietnam—as was my 1972 opponent, Richard Nixon.

After the turbulent 1968 Democratic National Convention in Chicago, where it was obvious that this spirit of wide embrace was missing both inside and outside the convention hall, I was asked to chair the Democratic Party's Commission on Party Structure and Delegate Selection to make sure that, going forward, our delegates included not just middle-aged white men but women, minorities, and young people—any of the millions of Americans who felt they were outsiders to the political decision-making process. Although accomplishing that goal did not help me win the 1972 election, we unified our previously splintered party, paving the way for the Democratic administrations of Jimmy Carter, Bill Clinton, and Barack Obama.

In their bestselling book *The Emerging Demo-*

cratic Majority, authors John B. Judis and Ruy Teixeira note that despite my landslide loss, the '72 election presaged "a new Democratic majority in the twenty-first century." The authors note that while I lost the popular vote, I brought in several blocs, including nonwhite voters, women, college communities, youth, teachers, clergymen, and other professionals, who today are vital components of the Democratic Party.

As a stand-in candidate for Robert Kennedy after his assassination, I was in Chicago in 1968, when the Democratic Party's New Deal coalition fractured over the Vietnam War. From my fourth-floor suite in the Blackstone Hotel, I watched police officers close in on antiwar protesters. So it was momentous, in 2008, to see a far different Democratic coalition take the stage at Grant Park the night Barack Obama captured the election to become our nation's first African American president.

Because there are no official Democratic litmus tests—thank heavens!—this is one person's view of what it means to be a Democrat—or perhaps what I think a Democrat *ought* to be. No one can write a book like this that is not personal, that is not influenced by his own observations and experience. As a child, I disliked the revivalist preachers' flamboyant oratorical style, and to this day I flinch when I hear speakers—religious, political, or otherwise—rely on passion at the expense of logic.

I was greatly influenced by my parents, who were soft-spoken and measured. They were "Ye shall know them by their fruits" people. So I'm going to tell you as straightforwardly as possible what being a Democrat means to me.

Above all, being a Democrat means having compassion for others. It means putting government to work to help the people who need it. It means using all available tools to provide good health care and education, job opportunities, safe neighborhoods, a healthy environment, a promising future. It means standing up for people who have been kept down, whether they are Native Americans or African Americans, women, immigrants, or the homeless. It means taking care of the mentally ill, of seniors, of vulnerable children, of veterans—and making sure all people are treated with respect and dignity.

There has never been a more critical time in our nation's history to rely on these fundamental Democratic principles. We are at a crossroads over how the federal government in Washington and state legislatures and city councils across the land allocate their financial resources. Which fork we take will say a lot about Americans and our values. A budget, whether for a family, a Girl Scout troop, a family-owned hamburger franchise, or the entire federal government, is an expression of priorities. And expenditures I consider essential to keep our country great do not line up with the Republicans' view, especially since they have been all but overtaken from within by extremists known as the Tea Party. Movement supporters are fueled by a desire to drastically reduce the size and cut the purse strings of the federal government and to force states to be the motors that get things done. In the 2011 budget battle between President Barack Obama and the Democratic Senate on one side and the Republican-led House of Representatives on the other, the Department of Defense was about the only government agency alleged conservatives did not march to the guillotine. How deeply they would like to go is evidenced by Congress's decision to ax $504 million—about 7 percent—from the Women, Infants and Children (WIC) program developed by the Senate Select Committee on Nutrition and Human Needs (also known as the McGovern Committee), which I chaired from its establishment in 1968 until 1977. This valuable program provides food and infant formula to low-income mothers and their children through the age of five. As one of the senators who originally proposed WIC and saw it into law, I feel a father's pride that it has fed roughly 177 million low-income hungry children and mothers—and a father's grief that it has been so drastically cut.

I view the federal government differently not only from Republicans, but often from many Democrats. Born to teetotaling parents who disapproved of Franklin Roosevelt's support of the Twenty-first Amendment repealing Prohibition, I began to change my allegiance when I saw how FDR's bold initiatives—including Social Security, the Federal Deposit Insurance Corporation (FDIC), the Rural Electrification Act, the Works Projects Administration, and the Civilian Conservation Corps—stabilized the country and made hurting Americans whole again.

My sense of injustice crystallized when, as a ten-year-old boy, I saw our great family friend Art Kendall sitting on his back steps with tears running down his cheeks. I'm not sure that I had ever seen an adult cry, and this was especially shocking, because Art was a man's man—a tough, hardworking farmer, up long before dawn, who would stay awake through the night to help a sow give birth and who also knew his way around a shotgun during pheasant hunting season. He told my father that he had just gotten a check from the stockyard for a year's production of pigs. The check didn't cover the expense of transporting the livestock to market. Four years later, in 1936, U.S. senator Peter Norbeck—a much loftier South Dakota Republican than I was back then—endorsed President Roosevelt. When asked why, Norbeck said:

"Because I think nine-cent hogs under Roosevelt are better than three-cent hogs under Hoover."

President Roosevelt's programs were sufficiently effective, as was his leadership during World War II, for him to secure four terms in the White House and for the United States to emerge as the greatest military and economic engine on earth.

Today we need only look around to understand why a progressive federal government can be a powerful force for good. We need a vigorous and alert Food and Drug Administration to assure that our food supply is safe and that our medications help keep us well instead of making us sick. We need to protect our tallest trees and our tiniest endangered species. We need to safeguard the air we breathe and the water we drink. We need to plan for the future by developing alternative sources of energy to lessen our dependence on foreign oil. And yes, we need a strong national defense. (What we don't need are unnecessary wars in Vietnam, Iraq, and Afghanistan that kill or cripple our young men and now women. These wars are the chief cause of our federal deficits and debt.)

Besides performing these routine duties, we need a government that is prepared to come to our aid in times of disaster. In 1995 the Federal Emergency Management Agency (FEMA) under Bill Clinton led a robust relief effort after the Oklahoma City bombing. Ten years later, after Hurricane Katrina struck New Orleans, the same agency, weakened by George W. Bush, was slow to respond to the dismal conditions inside that city's convention center, causing people who had already lost their homes, their livelihoods, and their loved ones to suffer even more. I've noticed that Republicans who complain about the size and scope of the federal government never seem to mind this same government's money going to aid in relief and rebuilding efforts after tornadoes, floods, and other calamities. The governors of Florida, Alabama, Louisiana, and Mississippi did not ask the federal government to stay away as oil from the BP spill gushed into the Gulf of Mexico.

Despite President Obama's leadership, the Tea Party's narrow, negative mentality is gaining ground and influencing the GOP at the very time we should be taking the opposite approach to our nation's problems and helping our fellow citizens.

In the following chapters I will lay out my vision of how to restore our nation to health, drawing on core values that define the Democratic Party.

All Americans believe in the power of the individual to shape his personal destiny through hard work. But unlike Republicans, we Democrats do not believe in blinding ourselves to the challenges that our fellow citizens may be facing in life, sometimes through no fault of their own.

To me, Republicans are like the residents of a well-to-do community where the streets are safe, the children healthy, the living easy. They wish to sit behind high walls and congratulate themselves on the good fortune they and their families enjoy.

They deliberately choose to isolate themselves from their fellow citizens outside the fortress: the unemployed steel worker whose job has been outsourced to China, who cannot support his family and needs retraining; the struggling single mother who works two jobs but who cannot afford afternoon and evening child care to keep her kids safe when the school day ends; the immigrant landscape worker swindled into taking out a mortgage he could never afford; the rural grandmother on Social Security raising grandchildren who have lost their parents to the fastest-growing drug epidemic in America, crystal meth; the millions of Americans who have been driven to declare bankruptcy because of a loved one's cancer or chronic illness.

We Democrats believe people should be allowed to enjoy the fruits of their hard labor, but we know that a two-tiered economy, where CEOs rake in billions for laying off their fellow citizens, is neither fair nor sustainable. A society built on economic injustice cannot grow. Underlying the Republican agenda is a desire to turn back the clock to the world before the New Deal, returning us to what FDR so eloquently described as the two Americas.

I will address how we can solve issues like joblessness; the war in Afghanistan; the unbridled greed on Wall Street; our failure to educate the young; the staggering fact that nearly 17 million American children go to bed hungry; our national crisis of self-confidence triggered by 9/11; the toll the terrible addictions to alcohol and drugs takes on our families, our economy, and our nation; the loss of civility in politics and elsewhere; the deliberate mistruths about taxes and President Obama; and the growing-uglier-by-the-minute media environment.

I offer my thoughts with the understanding that no one will agree with everything I say. That is okay. Democrats represent a party of ideas, with the common goal of harnessing federal power to serve the public interest. What unites us is our desire to propel our great country onward by meeting the needs of the many, in addition to the few who have it made. A guiding belief for Democrats is that we bring everyone along in a growing economy and an improving society.

I want to hark back to the words that mean the

most to me as an American: Abraham Lincoln's appeal in his first inaugural address to "the better angels of our nature."

I am optimistic. It's a habit of mine to not get down on the things I care passionately about: our country, world peace, and the St. Louis Cardinals. One always has to believe that things will get better. We have faced worse challenges—the Civil War, the Great Depression, World War II, the Cold War with the Soviet Union—yet somehow this great nation always seems to stumble forward.

COMPASSION

First and foremost, a modern-day Democrat believes in a dynamic federal government sensitive to public need and direction. In recent years, many of those who call themselves conservatives have begun to brand the federal government as the enemy. With this hostile view of the government in mind, its critics oppose such programs as Social Security, Medicare, and veterans' benefits. They also oppose such time-tested democratic systems as the graduated income tax.

In contrast, a Democrat strongly believes in such programs and regards the federal government not as the enemy but as a friendly partner. As one who has traveled the globe since my military service in World War II, I have witnessed no government as good as the United States of America's. We have the best civil service in the world. We have the best foreign service. We have the best military. Do these agencies sometimes make mistakes? Of course. They are made of human beings. But as an American and as a Democrat, I'm proud to honor the federal government. I was pleased to serve that government in World War II, helping to bring down Hitler, Tojo, and Mussolini, who threatened to destroy our democratic way of life. I was gratified to serve South Dakota and the nation for nearly a quarter of a century in the U.S. Congress. It was my high privilege to serve as President Kennedy's Food for Peace director and later as President Clinton's ambassador to the Food and Agriculture Organization (FAO) of the United Nations in Rome.

It is a source of gratitude and pride that in all these posts I served the federal government. I took only one oath: to uphold the Constitution of the United States.

The reason our Constitution is so strong is that

it had good authors: George Washington, Benjamin Franklin, James Madison, Thomas Jefferson, John Adams, Alexander Hamilton, and John Jay. Perhaps when we feel down on the follies of Congress and the national government—and there *are* such follies—we would be well advised to think of some of the wise programs emanating from Washington: rural electrification, the school lunch program, the interstate highways, Medicare, Social Security, the national parks, national defense, and many others.

So, what does it mean to be a Democrat beyond seeing the federal government as an instrument of building a better society?

During my years in Congress and for the four decades since, I've been labeled a "bleeding-heart liberal." It was not meant as a compliment, but I gladly accept it. My heart does sometimes bleed for those who are hurting in my own great country and abroad.

A bleeding-heart liberal, by definition, is someone who shows enormous sympathy toward others, especially the least fortunate. Well, we ought to be stirred, even to tears, by society's ills. And sympathy is the first step toward action. Empathy is born out of the old biblical injunction "Love thy neighbor as thyself."

My empathetic nature is a gift from my mother, Frances McLean, and my father, the Reverend Joseph McGovern, a pastor of the Wesleyan Methodist church. We followed the path set by its founder, John Wesley, who believed that it was our responsibility to show compassion for the homeless, the sick, the vulnerable; for miners and factory workers. From my earliest days, that message—which, at its center, is about basic human compassion—took root deep in my soul. It's ironic that, while my parents were Republicans, the values they instilled in me made me a Democrat. I might add that in Republican South Dakota I was repeatedly elected to high office by winning nearly all the Democratic voters and one-third of the Republicans.

A good Democrat feels genuine concern for our fellow human beings and for all living creatures. This means helping people who are too old or too young or too infirm to take care of themselves. It means speaking out on behalf of people who are so financially stretched they cannot afford heat—or they have to make an untenable choice between buying food or medicine. It means not giving the wealthy tax breaks at the expense of the middle class. It means refusing to turn Medicare into a voucher program, kill Head Start, or abandon nutrition programs for the elderly poor. We Democrats do not shun our responsibility to assist the unemployed, the physically or mentally ill, the hungry or the homeless. We do not oppose pay raises for our military at a time when many enlisted soldiers are dependent on food stamps to feed their families.

Just as Franklin Roosevelt restored hope to millions of Americans who lost their jobs, their homes, and their life savings during the Depression, it is part of our Democratic mandate to help those in trouble. We are the party behind Social Security, Medicare, and Medicaid. We are the party of Franklin Roosevelt's New Deal, John Kennedy's New Frontier, and Lyndon Johnson's Great Society.

I went into public service to help those who struggle, to fight for people who had no one to fight for them, to see that the poor had a fair shot at earning a decent wage. That's what Democrats stand for.

And over time, I have learned that empathy for our fellow man is not only the moral response, it is often, ultimately, less costly.

I saw compassion at work at the end of World War II. I was in the Fifteenth Air Force and had just completed the thirty-five combat missions that all Army Air Corps pilots were required to fly. If we survived, we would be sent back to the States. It was June 1945, and the war ended just a few days after I was done. But our commander, General Nathan Farragut Twining (he went on to become chairman of the Joint Chiefs of Staff), sent down a memo directing us to leave behind the food, clothing, and medicine in our kits for the Europeans, who had lost everything. He asked for volunteers to fly the supplies up to northern Europe. The previous March, I had received a cable that my wife, Eleanor, had given birth to a little girl, Ann Marian. At war's end Ann was three months old.

I was anxious to return home to my young family, to meet our new baby. But I volunteered for the humanitarian mission. It was the right thing to do. In some cases we were bringing food to people we had been bombing a short time ago.

The Europeans I met were enormously grateful. I came to think of our supply flights as a miniature version of the European Recovery Program, forever known as the Marshall Plan, named after Franklin Roosevelt's chief wartime military adviser, Secretary of State George C. Marshall. Launched in 1948 with the bipartisan support of a Democratic president, Harry S. Truman, and a Republican Congress, the Marshall Plan gave $13 billion in economic aid to Europe; in the context of a total U.S. economy of just $258 billion, it was a hefty sum. Knowing we had fulfilled our moral obligation to help restore the countries decimated by the war—including our former enemies—I took great pride in America.

The Marshall Plan was a national act of compassion. It was also instrumental in shaping a more peaceful, prosperous, and democratic Western

Europe, and especially in establishing indelible bonds with Germany.

Looked at from a bottom-line perspective, the Marshall Plan was indeed expensive. But when we contrast the post–World War II period with the aftermath of World War I, it seems a small price. In 1918, Republicans opposed Democratic president Woodrow Wilson's blueprint for a League of Nations. The harsh way in which the victors dealt with Germany spawned the popular rage that brought Adolf Hitler to power, ultimately leading to World War II and the holocaust of six million Jews.

So compassion does more than make people feel good; it is a smart way to approach the world.

By the time I became a senator in 1963, our involvement in Vietnam was escalating steadily. I strongly opposed this war, and in 1965, after the first combat troops were deployed, I went on a fact-finding trip to Southeast Asia to make sure that my position was well-founded. At a military hospital, I met brave young American soldiers, each of whom was a victim of sniper fire or of a land mine that took a leg, an arm, a face. The men's stories devastated me, especially since they were really boys still. I got special permission to stop at a civilian hospital in Da Nang, where I saw hundreds of bloodied and bandaged Vietnamese men, women, and children lying about on the hospital grounds, the front porch, and, sometimes, two to a cot in a ward. All had been wounded by shrapnel from American bombs.

These were key experiences in making the withdrawal of United States military forces out of Vietnam my "magnificent obsession," as a member of my Senate staff once called it. For a decade, until our last soldier left in 1975, the war was at the top of my mind. By the end of the war, 58,000 Americans, two million Vietnamese, two million Cambodians, and two million Laotians died in the conflict. My anguish over our continuing involvement in that faraway country was the driving force of my public career.

Another preoccupation of mine has been feeding the hungry. In 1957, as a fledgling U.S. congressman of a farming state then known for corn, wheat, and pigs, it didn't make sense to me that our nation's surplus wheat was piling up in American storage facilities while millions of people—some down the street, others continents away—went without food. A few years later I got the opportunity to do something about this profound disparity. As director of the Food for Peace program under President John F. Kennedy, it was my job to distribute excess food from U.S. farms to people in need at home and abroad. Again, in the late 1990s, as U.S. ambassador to the United Nations Food and Agriculture Organization, my goal was to reduce the number of hungry people around the world, a project I continued when Bob Dole, my good friend from the Senate and a Republican, supported my appointment as U.N. ambassador on world hunger.

But you need no official title to be compassionate. If you are concerned about your health, be concerned about the health of all Americans. If you are concerned about quality education for your children, how can you not be vocal about a quality education for all children? At a time when many Americans are an emergency-room visit or a broken transmission away from financial catastrophe, it is incumbent upon us to create a cushion by extending Medicare to all Americans, making sure we pay a living wage, and skewing income taxes toward those who earn the most money. I don't mean this as a punitive measure. As Democrats, we must support policy that is fair for all. We must resist the desire to do what is best for ourselves at the expense of those with less. Americans deserve leaders who put the voters first, which is something the GOP doesn't do. It's why it stuns me each time I hear of another election in which blue-collar workers have voted Republican—against their own economic self-interest.

Many Americans have lost faith. Social mobility—the ability to advance from one class to the next—has been such a defining characteristic of our country that it has its own shorthand: the American Dream. But two of its key components, a college education and owning a home, are becoming more difficult for many people to achieve. While 63 percent of Americans are optimistic about their family's future over the next fifty years, according to the Pew Research

Center, this is a significant drop from the 81 percent who felt that way in 1999.

This falloff in confidence is understandable. We hear near-daily reports of questionable or illegal corporate dealings and cover-ups, the erosion of workers' rights, and the news that the wealthiest 1 percent of our population gained 24 percent of the nation's income. In 2010 thirty-two companies compensated their top executives more than they paid in corporate income taxes. Companies that laid off thousands of workers or were rescued by government bailouts are paying their CEOs and other top executives annual multimillion-dollar bonuses.

This erosion of the American way of life began in 1981, when Ronald Reagan became president. The GOP began dismantling the New Deal policies that spawned a thriving middle class. I bear no animosity toward Republicans, but I have learned, sadly, that working toward a common good is not usually their party's goal. Too often, their aim is protecting corporate interests.

Remember "compassionate conservatism," George W. Bush's catchphrase in his bid for the White House in 2000? He eventually stopped talking about it. My guess is that was because he had his hands full launching two wars—or because he realized that the precarious balancing act he had set for himself was impossible to carry out, given the constraints of his party's ideology. You can't say you want to help immigrants and then step up efforts to prosecute them, as Bush did. You can't say you want to help the middle class and then focus your tax cuts on the wealthy, as Bush did. You can't say you want to help seniors and then try to link Social Security to the stock market, as Bush did. And can you imagine what a disaster that would have been during our latest recession?

There was nothing compassionate about the fact that real wages failed to grow during Bush's tenure as president. People were borrowing—amassing greater household debt—just to maintain the same quality of life, just to run in place!

John A. Boehner, the Republican Speaker of the

House, is known for weeping when he speaks of his hardscrabble childhood, but over the course of more than two decades as a legislator, Boehner has consistently nixed legislation that would have made it easier for others to get a toehold into the American Dream. He has voted against increasing the minimum wage, voted against unemployment benefits, voted against student aid. Yet I'm told that as an individual he is a reasonable, good man in the eyes of both Republicans and Democrats.

I do not say that Democrats' openhanded approach to humankind is wholly selfless. We like getting ahead as much as anyone. But we realize that we are only as strong as the weakest among us. That's why we are the party of compassion.

FEAR AND DEFENSE
SPENDING

Everyone remembers what they were doing on September 11, 2001, when the news came that a plane had crashed into the north tower of the World Trade Center, followed minutes later by a crushing blow to its twin. I was in Paris, finishing lunch with the editors of the *International Herald Tribune* in my capacity as U.S. ambassador to the United Nations Food and Agriculture Organization when we got the first sickening reports. I was preparing to depart on a mission to Africa. As the events of the day unfolded, I recall thinking that the situation seemed in a number of ways far worse than the bombing of Pearl Harbor. I was just nineteen on

December 7, 1941, when an announcer broke into the New York Philharmonic radio broadcast I was listening to for my college music appreciation class. There were many more casualties in that attack. But Hawaii wasn't yet a state. Few Americans even knew where it was.

Watching the horrific events of 9/11 was an unimaginable shock to the American psyche. A *New York Times* editorial on September 12, 2001, described the previous morning as a time "in which history splits, and we define the world as 'before' and 'after.'"

Many years later, we still inhabit that "after" world. It is a world with color-coded alert levels, complex security procedures in government and office buildings, bomb-sniffing dogs, and public announcements about unattended bags. Since 9/11, we've had the shoe bomber; the underwear bomber; the Fort Hood, Texas, shooting rampage; the failed car bombing in New York's Times Square; and about three dozen other attempted terrorist attacks in the United States alone.

But even with these myriad threats, I believe we

have overemphasized the danger we're in. We live with too much fear and not enough common sense. The whole silliness of our response is exemplified by what has happened at our airports. Once sources of architectural pride, air terminals are now barricaded behind concrete. Inside, we are required to remove our shoes and belts, hand over our gels and liquids, and submit to body scans—with the ante being raised each time there's a new scare. What upsets me the most is when I see an elderly woman trying her darnedest to comply with these ridiculous rules, as if she could possibly be harboring an explosive in her toothpaste.

Now that our initial distress over 9/11 has dissipated, I suggest that we stop this needless hassle, a palliative that costs $7 billion a year and rising. To my mind, in fact, the entire Homeland Security department—with its more than 200,000 employees and more than $42 billion budget—ought to be dissolved. The third largest Cabinet department, behind Defense and Veterans Affairs, it sprang from 9/11's shock waves to put the agencies that deal with counterterrorism, including airport safety, under one roof.

I believe we should leave the business of protecting the American public from terrorist attacks to the FBI, the CIA, and our police departments. (The FBI has a vibrant counterterrorism branch but somehow manages to stay independent.) But I suspect that of all the discretionary funds Congress could swing its scythe at, it will not fell the Homeland Security behemoth. Why? Its very existence makes us feel safer.

We are a nation in which fear and paranoia run deep. Since the Pilgrims made landfall in 1620, we have burned so-called witches at the stake, hauled Japanese-Americans to internment camps, and black-listed people who we labeled Communists. It's as though we are never without an enemy, whether from within or without, real or imagined.

The purpose of terrorism is to knock people off balance. We don't need to do the perpetrators' work by terrifying ourselves, by looking for a bogeyman in every closet. But we have done exactly that. As Walt Kelly's famous cartoon character Pogo said in 1970, "We have met the enemy and he is us."

In my lifetime, I believe Republicans have fomented popular fears to their best advantage. Only after Senator Joseph McCarthy, a Republican from Wisconsin, took his finger-pointing too far—accusing the Army of being infiltrated by Communists—did his influence wane. In the meantime, he fanned our anxieties to the point that Americans were imagining a Soviet spy or sympathizer behind every tree.

But that wasn't the end of the GOP's fear factor. In 1968, Richard Nixon's "law and order" mantra played subtly on southern whites' racial concerns. Ronald Reagan's wedge issue? "Cadillac-driving welfare queens." George H. W. Bush's? Willie Horton. In 2002, George W. Bush and Dick Cheney sounded the 9/11 Klaxon to persuade Congress that we needed to invade Iraq. Two years later their entire reelection strategy was based on scare tactics. "The Democrat approach in Iraq comes down to this," President Bush said. "The terrorists win and America loses." For the record, there is not one thing that makes me angrier than the insinuation that I—or my fellow Demo-

crats—are less patriotic than our Republican breth-
ren. I would put my life on the line for our country any
time, just as I did in World War II.

I was awarded the Distinguished Flying Cross for
flying on thirty-five bombing raids over Europe during the Second World War. I didn't wait to be drafted.
I enlisted in the Army Air Corps a few weeks after
Pearl Harbor. The reason I wanted to become a combat pilot was because, even after taking a civilian
pilot-training program, I hadn't been able to shake
my fear of flying. I was determined to conquer it.

But I have noticed that a lot of people who beat
their chests have never been near a military plane or a
battlefield; they've never heard a bullet pass an inch
above their skulls. They've never seen a buddy in arms
gasping his way to death. Sometime in the late 1960s,
as I had the floor trying to make the case against our
continuance in Vietnam, a fellow senator stood up
and said, "I stand with our troops. As long as I hold
this seat, I stand with the troops."

I said, "You're not standing with our troops.
They're in Vietnam. You're in the Senate, with air-

conditioning, mahogany paneling, and pages to run your errands for you. Neither of us is standing with our troops." I added: "The best service we can render to the boys and youth we have sent into a mistaken war is to bring them home." The visitors up in the gallery are not supposed to applaud, but they did and I was grateful to them. I can still hear that clapping.

In those days I was against the national draft, and I called repeatedly to end it. But several years after the Vietnam War was over, my close friend Ted Kennedy, the late Massachusetts senator, led me to reconsider.

I still don't believe we should enact a draft in peacetime, but I think anytime Americans are involved in military operations, we ought to have a draft. It's only fair that all of us go to some risk in time of war. We shouldn't leave that to people who are too poor to make a living any other way. It's a national disgrace that working-class kids join the military to get their shot at the American Dream by qualifying for the GI Bill, which helps pay for college, while the kids who have enjoyed the most from our society are the least likely to serve our nation. Second, if the children of our country's leaders were serving in the military—if upper-middle-class kids were being drafted out of Harvard and Smith—we might never enter unwise wars like those we're in now or were in for so many years in Vietnam.

In talking about the Republican provocation of fear, I do not question that there are serious threats to the United States today. That is beyond dispute. The 9/11 attack opened many eyes to the hatred on the part of zealous young Muslims against America and all that we stand for—a sentiment that Osama bin Laden was able to seize upon and organize against us. And even though bin Laden is now dead, the underlying hostility still exists. But I wonder about our exaggerated reaction to the physical danger. The Patriot Act invades our privacy at home, while abroad we continue to be engaged in an unfounded war against Afghanistan. And despite President Obama's drawdown, we continue to have 46,000 U.S. troops in Iraq. None of these things will make us safer. They simply take away money we dearly need to address other national priorities.

The only thing that has been more self-destructive than the money we've wasted on the Homeland Security department's massive bureaucracy has been our overspending on defense. Our military budget is loaded with needless but frighteningly expensive over-kill. It gobbles up tax money that is urgently needed in other parts of our national life. We skimp on education, health care, renewable energy, and clean water and air. (Sometimes our diplomacy is as witless as our defense spending. A clear example of diplomatic folly is our sixty-year boycott of Cuba and refusal to recognize her diplomatically. Although Cuba is a small island with almost no military, we have refused to carry on any relations with the Cubans. This has been the case since Fidel Castro overthrew the corrupt dictator Fulgencio Batista in 1959. Batista had been in bed with the Mafia gangsters who ran the nightlife of gambling and sex in Havana.)

Each year our war machine claims the largest discretionary portion of the federal budget. I was heartened by President Obama's acknowledgment of this reality in his June 2011 TV address to the nation, when he said: "Over the last decade, we have spent a trillion dollars on war, at a time of rising debt and hard economic times. Now, we must invest in America's greatest resource—our people." I couldn't have agreed more when he said, "America, it is time to focus on nation building here at home."

As anyone who followed my political career knows, I have never believed that endless military spending was the right course.

On August 2, 1963, in my second speech as a freshman senator, I took the floor to oppose our involvement in Vietnam. I called for lowering the then $50 billion military budget by $5 billion—a huge amount in 1963 dollars. "Have we not remembered that the defense of a great nation depends not only upon the quality of its arms, but also on the quality of its economic, political, and moral fabric?" I asked.

"Is the size of our military budget the chief criterion of effective international leadership and national strength in today's world?"

Fervently believing the answer to both of my questions was—and still is—no, I continued to call for a reduction in military spending each year until I left the Senate in 1981, swept out by the Republican tide that brought Ronald Reagan into the White House. But my efforts were hardly more than a futile exercise. When the Soviet leader Mikhail Gorbachev and Reagan agreed to a broad nuclear disarmament concept, it marked the beginning of the end of the Cold War. Already the United States had done away with the Cold War–era formula known as the "two-and-a-half-war doctrine," which provided us with a military strong enough to take on the Soviet Union, China, and a lesser country simultaneously, should the need arise. But even with those reductions, the outcome is the same: we still have far more deterrence capabilities than we need. Indeed, I know of no country that is spoiling for war with the United States or wants to invade our shores. These days, if we want a war we have to send our soldiers into some other country.

The U.S. defense budget now stands at $700 billion (a figure that includes our nuclear weapons program and the supplemental costs of executing two wars), the highest it has been since World War II, adjusting for inflation—and about as much as the total of the world's other nations' military budgets combined. It consumes roughly half of our nation's discretionary spending. So it's curious to me that Tea Party extremists who want to reduce the federal government target infant formula, job training, and medical research rather than the Department of Defense. As I write, Republican congressman Paul Ryan's "Path to Prosperity" budget calls for a 3 percent cut, or $22 billion, in the Pentagon budget. It would take five times that—$120 billion—just to bring it back to what it was under President Clinton. President Obama's initial request for 2012 was $680 billion, or 51 percent of all U.S. discretionary spending, meaning that his baseline budget would go up even as the cost of prosecuting our wars falls.

You might be surprised to find that my role model for setting military spending is neither a liberal nor a Democrat. It is Dwight David Eisenhower, a Republican who was elected president after serving as the Supreme Allied Commander during World War II. His farewell address, given at the White House, was shorter and less polished than the better-known inauguration speech that John F. Kennedy delivered from the U.S. Capitol's East Portico three days later. But Eisenhower's vision of the future, while more ominous, was more prescient than JFK's soaring words.

As President Eisenhower explained, the Cold War years were the first in which the United States had a permanent armaments industry. "We can no longer risk emergency improvisation of national defense," he said. But just as George Washington cautioned against foreign entanglements in 1796, Eisenhower reminded Americans that we "must guard against the acquisition of unwarranted influence, whether sought or unsought, by the military-industrial complex."

I am told that in an earlier draft of his speech, he used the more apt phrase "military-industrial-congressional complex," acknowledging the complicated role that the Senate and House of Representatives play in determining what the military can spend.

Cutting defense spending takes a measure of political will that my congressional colleagues could never muster. I understand why. First, each state has at least one military installation or factory producing military goods that provides jobs for constituents. Second, members of Congress do not want to give their political opponents an opening to brand them as "weak on defense." I had to answer that charge on more than one occasion in South Dakota. But self-preservation by politicians can lead to disaster, as it did in 2002 when the fear of looking "soft" on terrorism prompted Congress to approve of George W. Bush's wrongheaded war in Iraq. Iraq had absolutely nothing to do with the 9/11 attack, nor did Iraq have any nuclear weapons as Bush, Cheney, and Rumsfeld told us. They even brought General Colin Powell, then secretary of state, into this falsehood.

Presidents are certainly not immune to the impulse to look tough on military matters. President Reagan's weapons buildup was one of the hallmarks of his first term as president (along with his tax cuts). Any peace dividend we enjoyed under George H. W. Bush at the end of the Cold War did not last long. The defense budget rose again during the second term of Bill Clinton, who apparently wanted to establish an image as an unflinching leader beside a Republican Congress intent on impeaching him (one of the most ludicrous congressional efforts in American history). And in 2009, when President Obama agreed to a troop surge in Afghanistan, I believe he did so at least partly to send an unequivocal message that he was a commander in chief with a firm hand.

But there is more than one definition of "tough." We need to end the false choice between a bloated budget and a weak spine. Imagine what might have happened if more members of Congress had questioned President Bush's rush into Iraq. Thousands of lives might have been spared. And according to estimates by Nobel Prize–winning economist Joseph Stiglitz, $3 trillion in direct and indirect expenses might have been saved too. As for the Iraqis, our unjustified invasion and prolonged occupation smashed their country.

Do not mistake what I am saying. I do not want to strip this country of its military might. I understand that deterrence is vital to our well-being. But do we honestly think Iran or North Korea will launch a preemptive strike against the United States? Remember that our arsenal of fighter jets, battleships, submarines, and nuclear missiles did not stop nineteen al-Qaeda–trained men from bringing down four U.S. commercial airliners with box cutters and a few cans of Mace on 9/11.

I'm familiar with the argument that Osama bin Laden's death was a triumph of U.S. military might. But if you'll pardon the expression, I believe that is baloney. The cost of the small, hard-hitting, smooth-working squad of Navy SEALs that captured and killed bin Laden at his Pakistani compound was a minuscule fraction of the cost of the Afghan war. Our most symbolic victory was won by Special Ops, with a handful of men—not the 100,000 soldiers on the ground.

It seems that many Americans, especially Democrats, are finally losing their appetite for excessive military spending. An opinion poll by the Pew Research Center found that today just as many voters favor a decrease in military spending as favor an increase.

In a careful and convincing study, Lawrence Korb, a senior fellow at the Center for American Progress and a former assistant secretary of defense under President Reagan, and his associate Laura Conley have identified "unproven, over-budget, or strategically unnecessary" weapons and weapons programs that could be cut or canceled and not missed. Among them: the V-22 Osprey tilt-rotor aircraft. According to the study, the Osprey program has been plagued by so many technical problems since its 1991 inception that Dick Cheney, then secretary of defense, called it a "turkey." Rejecting the Navy's request for twenty-four new Ospreys would save $9.1 billion. Also: cut procurement of the Navy and Marine F-35 Joint Strike Fighter variants. Since 2002, estimates of the lifetime operational costs of the F-35 have more than doubled to $1 trillion. Alternative fighter jets such as the F/A-18E/F Super Hornet continue to be effective in the Navy and the Marines, so cutting their variants while allowing the Air Force to keep its entire buy would control spiraling costs without compromising American air superiority. Savings: $16.43 billion by 2015.

Beyond the cost of needless tanks and submarines are our unnecessary expenditures on personnel. It is well past time to bring home our troops not only from Iraq and Afghanistan but also from Western Europe and South Korea. Hitler has been dead for more than sixty years. The Korean conflict ended in 1953. These onetime theaters of war, where our forces number 120,000 and 29,000, respectively, no longer need to use the United States as their policemen.

I'm reminded of the slogan I used in my 1972 campaign, "Come Home, America"—a mantra we borrowed from Martin Luther King Jr. The idea was to bring the electorate back to the values upon which our nation was founded. Now I believe that same catchphrase is applicable in a different context: it is time to bring our troops home and tend to the pressing domestic matters we have overlooked for far too long. President Obama has announced a 10,000-troop withdrawal from Afghanistan in 2011, with a second withdrawal of 23,000 soldiers in 2012. It's a start. But why are we not bringing them all home, right now?

In the tradition of President Eisenhower's farewell address, Admiral Michael Mullen, outgoing chairman of the Joint Chiefs of Staff—the nation's senior military officer—has warned that our mounting national debt is weakening our economy so much that it is the single biggest threat to national security. By overemphasizing defense, we weaken other sources of our national strength: the quality of our children's education, the health of our citizenry, and our stewardship of the environment. No one decision will solve all of our problems, but by making the cuts I've suggested and others according to the Korb-Conley study I mentioned before, we can save more than a trillion dollars in the current decade.

It is time for Democrats—and for all Americans—to acknowledge that we are well past a place of diminishing returns. A generation ago, under far different circumstances, the Soviet Union spent so much on its arms buildup against the United States that its economy collapsed. As an old history professor, I am wondering if perhaps there is not a lesson in there for us. Being the strongest country on earth doesn't mean much if our citizens cannot find worthwhile jobs or affordable housing, quality schools, good health care, and a clean environment.

THE PURPOSE
OF GOVERNMENT

Growing up in Mitchell, South Dakota, in the 1920s, I remember a parishioner coming to my father's parsonage and condemning income taxes. My father, a Republican, nonetheless said, "Brother Smith, if you're paying high income taxes, it means you're making a lot of income, so praise the Lord!"

I could understand the man's surprise, because the modern income tax system, established in 1913, hadn't been around very long at that point. Still, my father's response made sense to me then, and it still does.

It always annoys me when people recite that tired chestnut about death and taxes, with taxes coming out as the less desirable option. When I came home from Europe after World War II, tax rates were much higher than they are now (from 1950 to 1963 the marginal tax rate on the wealthiest Americans topped 90 percent). It was a time of enormous change in our country: we established the Marshall Plan (officially, the European Recovery Act) in Europe, broke ground for America's new Interstate Highway System, and, with the help of the GI Bill, enabled veterans to go to college and buy their first homes. I was proud to help support the growth happening all around me.

Today I put taxes in the same category as paying a mechanic to change the oil in my car, a handyman to clean the gutters on my house, or a cardiologist to check the condition of my heart. I spend money on these services and products, because that's what it takes to maintain a life in which the things I depend on—car, gutters, ventricles, to name a few—work properly.

It's the same when I send a check to the Internal Revenue Service each April. In return, I get such necessities as air traffic control, the defense of our borders, clean water, a safe food supply, health care, pristine national parks—the list is long. Because my taxes help not only me, my children, and my grandchildren but also other families, I can't help but think that whatever I pay, it's the best investment I make.

I often feel that the federal government is more sensible about spending than I am. Like other consumers, I sometimes buy clothes I don't need, a new car when the old one runs fine, or a new TV because it's wider, it's flatter, or it has a sharper image than the model in my living room. I've always believed the United States is the greatest country on earth, and yet, in some cases, we're taxed far less than our European counterparts: in 2009, the average U.S. wage earner paid 29.4 percent in income taxes and Social Security compared to 49.2 percent in France, 50.9 percent in Germany, and 32.5 percent in the U.K.

But my confidence in our government is not naive.

I know that its workers can be wasteful and inept; that its programs can suffer duplication, ineffectiveness, and inertia; that it is susceptible to cheating and fraud. These are challenges that we can and must address. But I am also sure that our national government does far, far more good than harm. As the late Ted Sorensen, a personal friend, best known as President Kennedy's legendary speechwriter and special adviser, wrote in *Why I Am a Democrat*: "When government is honest, efficient, and democratically representative of the people's will . . . it can be an indispensable means by which society can improve itself, curb the inevitable ills, excesses, and injustices of the private sector and improve the human condition and sense of community for all."

And while Republicans love to point out the superiority of the free market, it's important to remember that just as government is far from infallible, so too do private enterprises fail us from time to time. Think Bernie Madoff and Enron, just for starters.

I believe that government and business work best

when they work together. In 2008, as in 1929, it was too little government regulation—not too much—that led to the subprime mortgage crisis and the unraveling of our banking system, the reverberations of which nearly brought down the global economy. And it was the government, in the form of the Troubled Asset Relief Program (TARP), aimed at financial institutions deemed "too big to fail," that helped Wall Street come roaring back, although Main Street continues to sputter.

According to the *Wall Street Journal,* in 2009, Wall Streeters—executives, investment bankers, traders, and money managers at thirty-eight top financial companies—earned $145 billion, a gain of 18 percent over their 2008 earnings of $123.4 billion and a 6 percent increase over the $137.23 billion paid out in 2007, a record year. Contrast this leap with the 1 percent gain made between 2007 and 2009 in the real median earnings of full-time, year-round male workers. Women's income in the same period did not grow at all.

I believe that Americans generally want our government to be strong, active, and creative in dealing with our problems. That's why the New Deal generation was so enthusiastic about Franklin Roosevelt's initiatives to end the Depression. He put young men to work, created Social Security to give older Americans a cushion against poverty, powered up the Tennessee Valley Authority, and safeguarded our bank deposits.

FDR's Rural Electrification Administration is one of my favorite examples of government ingenuity. In the 1910s and 1920s, because it didn't make good business sense for private electric companies to put up power lines in sparsely populated areas, including parts of South Dakota, many families had to depend on lanterns when dusk came. As a boy I remember being scared when we were in the countryside after nightfall. (In truth, I don't know whether I was more anxious of the dark or of getting caught, since generally, when my friends and I were out at that time of day, it was to steal watermelons.) My personal situation aside, in the 1930s the federal government took up the electrification challenge and solved it handily, bringing power and light to people in remote places, from Alabama to Oregon. I know it made the farmers outside Mitchell feel a lot less lonely.

A good Democrat subscribes to the philosophy that strength comes from drawing together in this way to serve the collective good. The federal government is simply the conduit. As Teddy Roosevelt, a Republican and one of our most progressive presidents, said: "The government is us; we are the government, you and I."

But our federal government—you and I—has never been under more forceful attack from the right, especially by the Tea Party extremists, than now. My guess is that the movement is rooted in the anger of people who are not doing as well economically as they had hoped, who feel that life has not dealt with them in an encouraging way, and who are lashing out at the government, an easy target. Tea Party Republicans have convinced many people that Washington does not have their best interests at heart.

No matter the cause, the result is that the annual

wrangling over the federal budget—along with the discussions over tax reform and the national debt ceiling (the highest in our history) that are raging as I write—have so frayed the relationships between Democrats and Republicans in Congress that it is difficult to imagine how meaningful compromise can occur. Civility is at a new low in our politics and in much of the media as well.

How we resolve our dueling visions is of no small moment. The answers will determine not only who gets what share of the American pie but our very identity as a nation. It seems to me that our two political parties are separated by one of the largest chasms since the nation was divided on the expansion of slavery.

Democrats are not knee-jerk people who want a sprawling government for its own sake. Between 1933 and 1940, expenditures on Franklin Roosevelt's New Deal programs totaled just $7 billion each year, but that money rippled out to lift up millions of people. FDR was successful not because of how much he spent but because he was able to direct the government's power to serve the people—and he had a clear sense of what defined the nation's best interests.

What mattered to Democrats then and now is that we have an effective government—a government that keeps the social compact we established over the course of nearly four centuries, starting on board the *Mayflower*. When pioneer families headed west to settle new parts of our great land, life on the frontier could be unforgiving. But they didn't keep going if they saw another wagon in distress. They stopped to help fix the broken wheel. They didn't leave their parents behind on a hillside when they were no longer productive. They fed them and gave them a place to sleep.

Republicans celebrate the individual. But they forget the importance of community and generosity—the spirit that motivates a neighbor to lend a hand to the famer whose barn burned down in a lightning strike or the widow rearing a brood of hungry children because her husband died in a workplace accident. The frontier meant freedom and opportunity, but it also symbolized misfortune and trouble. We Democrats recognize this about the past and the present. This is the spirit that our party must now carry forward.

At our core, Democrats believe that it is the government's job—or, to paraphrase Teddy Roosevelt, yours and mine—to empower all of our citizens through health care and a good education, to give them the potential to become anything and everything they can be. Reasonable people can disagree on what type of help we should offer—and how much—when people are in trouble. But the underlying philosophy is this: help we must.

Today's Republicans, on the other hand, believe that the public is best served when it is hardly served at all. To quote Ted Sorensen once again, "In Republican eyes, government should be a clerk, not a leader."

The real truth is that the Republican view of government is not always impassive. Republicans, in fact, are aggressively supportive of government when it fits their thin purposes. They support telling Americans what to do in the bedroom. They support restrictions on individual privacy. They support limits on the judgments citizens can receive in the courts and the power of unions and workers' rights. They support tearing down the hallowed wall between church and state. They generally support withholding civil rights from gay Americans.

They even meddle in a person's right to die. Remember how, in 2005, the Republican Congress passed a bill to try to prevent Terri Schiavo's husband from taking her off a feeding tube even though she had been in a "persistent vegetative state"—unable to respond purposefully to any stimuli—for fifteen years? What was small-government about that?

I think of the differences between the parties this way: Democratic thinkers have an appreciation for what government can do and an equal respect for where it does not belong. Republicans insert government into areas where it should not venture—when it suits their business interests and moral claims.

But it's how Republicans and Democrats are shaping the 2012 budget that offers the starkest reminder of our dissimilarities. The Republican solution to the deficit problem is simple: cut billions of dollars in federally funded programs, from Medicaid and Medicare to clean energy and student financial aid.

Their excuse? The fact that we have hit our national debt ceiling—the total amount of money the federal government can borrow from itself and from U.S. and foreign investors. They say we must either raise the limit or default on our financial obligations. Never before has raising the debt limit been equated to the end of the world. Since 1962, Congress has raised it more than seventy times (including ten times in the past ten years). But in a game of political brinksmanship, the Republican-led House of Representatives insisted on budget cuts that *exceeded* the debt limit increase—and framed it as the Democrats' fault if we could not meet their demands and, in the end, had to default on our national obligations. And the battle still wages.

It is interesting to note that while Republicans blame Democrats for taxing and spending our way into an unsustainable situation, the first dramatic increase in our debt occurred during the eight years of Ronald Reagan's presidency. It was a period of sizable tax cuts matched only by his spending spree to accelerate the arms race against the Soviet Union. If President Reagan had cut federal spending in an amount roughly equivalent to the tax cuts he championed, he might have prevented deficit financing. Instead he added $4 trillion to the national debt.

I'm the first to say that piling on to the national debt is not a good idea in perpetuity. We have to pay it down as a share of our economy. We do not want to be beholden to creditors whose politics and, perhaps, agendas differ from our own. Nor do we want to add to the burden our children and grandchildren will shoulder. This is not some vague idea for me. I am a father of five children, the grandfather of twelve, and the great-grandfather of six. And yet, lowering the debt does not carry the urgency that many people have placed on it. With our economy's recovery in such a feeble state, gutting our social programs today simply for the sake of hitting an arbitrary target number is austerity for the sake of politics. It will cost us several hundred thousand jobs at the very moment that we are trying to make up for lost ground. It makes as much sense as putting a starving man on a low-calorie diet. It would be far better to enact deficit-reduction measures now that will not become effective for a couple of years—at the earliest. This would have the effect of stabilizing the debt within a reasonable time period.

In 1980, when George H. W. Bush opposed Ronald Reagan for the Republican nomination, he called Reagan's supply-side economic theory—the idea that a tax cut would stimulate the economy by freeing up more cash in the private sector—"voodoo economics." I have always had great respect for President Bush Sr. as a leader who knows the value of coalition building and compromise. Though he stopped criticizing Ronald Reagan's ideas early enough in the campaign to become his running mate, time has proved George H. W. Bush's original assessment to be correct.

But prescience on the part of the father did not stop his son, George W. Bush, from being seduced a generation later by Ronald Reagan's magical thinking. President Bush II was handed a balanced budget when he assumed the White House from Bill Clinton. Then, in the summer of 2001, before the events of 9/11 occurred and fear of terrorism—and thoughts of retribution—gripped the country, the slowing economy was Topic A in Washington. President Bush, his vice president, Dick Cheney, and the GOP Speaker of the House, Dennis Hastert, insisted that tax cuts were just what the country needed to jump-start spending and create jobs. When Congress passed the Economic Growth and Tax Relief Reconciliation Act of 2001, putting $300 to $600 back in the pockets of 95 million Americans, President Bush hailed it as "a victory for fairness and a vote for economic growth." But it's reasonable to say that from June 2001, when the cuts were signed into law, to June 2004, the tax cuts did not add a single job that wouldn't have been created otherwise. All told, only 4.7 million private-sector jobs were created in the six years between 2001 and 2007, when the recession began. Compare that to the 18.2 million new private sector jobs created between 1993, after Congress voted to increase taxes, and 2000, during Bill Clinton's presidency.

President Bush replicated Reagan's record in more ways than one. The combination of lowering revenues and increasing spending—primarily on two dubious wars, no less—added nearly $5 trillion to the national debt, which stood at well over $10 trillion when Barack Obama was sworn in as president.

The debt has risen rapidly under Barack Obama with good reason: he inherited the worst recession since the Great Depression. And with our tax revenues at just 16 percent of the total size of the economy, it's the least revenue we've collected in fifty years.

But this is not the time to sharpen our pencils; this is the time to raise our sights. Otherwise, how will we help our fellow Americans find jobs, stay in their homes, and get back on their feet?

And let me make this clear: deficit reduction cannot alone bring the budget into balance. Republicans have declared that "taxes are not on the table"—except, of course, on their own terms, by which they mean *lowering* the tax rate on the wealthiest Americans to 25 percent.

In 2010, President Obama extended the Bush tax cuts—a necessary evil, perhaps, that's costing $80 billion over two years—simply to secure what he really thought we needed: an extension of unemployment insurance. We should let these cuts expire on time in 2012 and enact significant tax reform that will broaden the tax base. It is time to close some egregious loopholes and curb tax subsidies. And it is time to raise rates moderately for the wealthiest Americans.

Although Republicans say higher tax rates on the wealthy would cripple economic growth, history does not support this claim. During the postwar period, as I mentioned earlier, the tax rate on the wealthiest was 91 percent—and GDP grew by 3.67 percent. Under Ronald Reagan, the patron saint of tax cutting and the Republican Party, GDP grew by only 3.47 percent. If a tax rate as high as 91 percent didn't stall the economy, why would a 36 percent rate do so?

I am sickened by the idea that instead of working alongside President Obama to solve these problems in a bipartisan way, congressional Republicans are trying to hold him hostage to the Department of Labor's dismal monthly job reports in hopes that they can unseat him in the next election. They don't want to fix things, they want to retake the White House, regardless of the cost; Senate minority leader Mitch McConnell of Kentucky, in fact, has gone on record saying that his number one goal is to render Barack Obama "a one-term president." Republican House majority leader Eric Cantor walked out of a debt-ceiling negotiation meeting over his refusal to raise taxes.

Never during my lifetime have I witnessed any president beset by the kind of narrow partisanship that has plagued President Obama. The American people elected him for his vision—of change, of hope, of compromise. This is what he came to Washington to carry out. These ideals have been trampled on by Republicans.

Democrats put the love of nation over the love of party. We are on the right side of this fight.

FOOD AND HUNGER

Feeding the hungry has been perhaps my most enduring and compelling passion.

My introduction to hunger—not the physical pangs you feel when you skip a meal but deep-down undernourishment—came when I was a child during the Great Depression. Young men who rode the rails looking for work sometimes jumped off the train just before the Mitchell, South Dakota, depot and knocked on our door, asking to trade chores for food. If these "hoboes"—often college dropouts who could no longer pay their tuition—arrived even close to mealtime, Dad wouldn't just hand them a sandwich, he'd invite them to come sit at the table with us. They ate ravenously, as though chewing were an inconvenience that slowed down the delivery process to their stomach.

A few years later, during World War II, I was leaning against the railing of my U.S. troopship as we entered the harbor in Naples, Italy, when I saw that the docks were lined with children. They were calling out "Hey, Joe" and clamoring for us to toss them candy. To me, flinging out a couple of Baby Ruth bars seemed harmless, but the captain broke in over the loudspeaker ordering us not to throw anything. A few days earlier, he said, soldiers on another military ship had done that and, as they scrambled for the treats, some of the children, near starvation, had fallen off the dock and drowned.

The desperation of that scene stayed with me for a long time. I made a promise to myself that if I ever got a chance to do something about hunger, I would. And sixteen years later the United States government gave me the opportunity.

In 1960, I was a congressman making a run for

the U.S. Senate when Jack Kennedy came to South Dakota to campaign for president. Earlier that day he had spoken at a national corn-picking contest in Sioux Falls before tens of thousands of midwestern farmers. He really laid an egg. He didn't know much about agriculture, and someone had written him an uninspired speech. He knew it wasn't good. It was raining. The wind was blowing. He was trying to hold on to his notes. Nixon had spoken to the same audience the day before and had roused them up.

My hometown, Mitchell, was the next stop for Kennedy. When we got on his plane, he said to me, "George, what the hell am I going to do? I've been told there are six thousand people waiting at the Corn Palace."

I said, "What I would do, Jack, is throw away the speech and walk out onstage without any notes. Just say, 'I think the farmers can do more for the cause of peace in the world than any other group of Americans, because food is strength, food is health, food is goodwill in a hungry world. If I'm elected president,

I'm going to take the Food for Peace program, name a full-time man to head it, and put him in the White House, where he'll be close to me.'"

Food for Peace was created during the Eisenhower administration to distribute surplus wheat, corn, and other U.S. farm staples to a billion people in Latin America, Africa, and Asia, and to foster new markets for our agricultural products. It was originally known as Public Law 480, or simply as "surplus disposal," and when I was elected to the House of Representatives in 1956, Senator Hubert Humphrey and I worked hard to give it a new name with some humanitarian oomph.

Kennedy's speech only lasted about four minutes, but he got a thunderous ovation. He wound up losing South Dakota (though I'm pretty sure he carried those 6,000 people in the Corn Palace) and I lost my Senate campaign. On the Friday after Election Day, Eleanor and I were at dinner at a neighbor's house in Mitchell. The phone rang, and I'll be darned if it wasn't Jack Kennedy. He said, "George, before you make any plans, come see me." On day number three of his thousand-day presidency, he put me in charge of Food for Peace. And with his strong backing, the program moved ahead with new energy.

Republicans have typically supported Food for Peace because it benefits farm states. Now under the State Department's USAID umbrella, it not only distributes food from every state in our nation to hungry people around the world but also uses American know-how to teach farmers improved planting and harvesting techniques and distributes free school lunches. To commemorate its fiftieth anniversary, a glossy booklet featured a quotation from then president George W. Bush, saying, "Across the earth, America is feeding the hungry. More than 60 percent of international food aid comes as a gift of the people of the United States . . ."

But as I write, I'm not sure how much of the program will survive the House Republicans' current budget-cutting extravaganza. And it's certainly not the only food or nutrition program they seem to want to take the guts out of.

Food and hunger are not partisan issues. They are

human issues. Eating is neither an add-on nor a luxury. It is, rather, one of the few basic needs we share, whether we're talking about Barack Obama or George W. Bush; a Japanese fisherman or a Somali herder; someone who lives in a Dallas mansion or someone who has no home at all. And historically Republicans and Democrats have been able to find broad agreement around food. (The real difference between the two parties in this regard, as fellow Democrat James Carville once maintained, is that Republicans serve better food at barbecues.)

The Senate Select Committee on Nutrition and Human Needs, which I established and chaired, was a case study in bipartisanship. In 1968, I was watching a CBS News special report called *Hunger in America* with my wife, Eleanor, and two of our daughters. It showed students who could not afford to buy lunch as they stood around the edges of the cafeteria, watching their classmates eat. I couldn't believe that I was on the Senate Agriculture Committee and had no idea that children who didn't have the money couldn't get a free lunch. So I went to the Senate floor the next day and made a motion to create the select committee.

Bob Dole, a fellow World War II vet and Midwesterner, was my committee's ranking Republican. We were often on opposite sides of the political debate, especially in 1972, when I ran for president and he headed the Republican National Committee for Richard Nixon. But we found common ground in food. We worked together not only to provide free or reduced-price lunches and breakfasts to poor children in this country but also to reform the Food Stamp Program. Hubert Humphrey joined us to cosponsor legislation establishing the Women, Infants and Children (WIC) nutrition program, which offers food, infant formula, and health care to poor mothers and their children. (Although WIC received a $504 million cut in the 2011 budget, House Republicans, dissatisfied with their first effort, set their sights on cutting $650 million more for 2012. According to the Center on Budget and Policy Priorities, this means that up to 350,000 more eligible women and children would lose access to the program's offerings.)

After we left the Senate, Bob and I continued to work together. In 2002 we pushed Congress to pass legislation that established a permanent international program to feed schoolchildren called the McGovern-Dole International Food for Education and Child Nutrition Program. We shared the World Food Prize in 2008.

Sure, the GOP has had some ridiculous food fights. In 1981, Ronald Reagan's administration tried, unsuccessfully, to reclassify ketchup and pickle relish from condiments to vegetables to save $1 billion in the subsidized lunch program—the one that Bob Dole and I had started.

I'm not going to spend time explaining why we need to worry about hunger and other food-related problems. But let me say this: whether the Republicans are with us or against us on this, allowing anyone to go hungry—either your next-door neighbor or someone who lives on the other side of the globe—is simply not a Democratic option.

And there is work to be done right now. In 2008, when the latest numbers were available, 44 million

Americans were "food insecure," meaning they often lack the money to buy enough food, according to the World Hunger Education Service. Similarly, in 2011, some 44 million Americans depended on food stamps each month, a 10 percent jump from 2010. In twenty-seven states, one of every seven people uses food stamps.

Internationally, a 2010 report by the Food and Agriculture Organization of the United Nations shows that worldwide, 925 million people—almost a billion!—are hungry, most of them in developing countries. Three and a half million children die every year from undernourishment. The global economic crisis and rising food prices have only made matters worse. And drought has left seven million people in Kenya, Ethiopia, and Somalia severely malnourished.

I've seen this type of wrenching hunger many times. My first mission during the year and a half I headed Food for Peace was in a village in northeastern Brazil. I went with Arthur M. Schlesinger Jr., JFK's special assistant, and a Brazilian economist named Celso Furtado. We walked into one hut where an emaciated woman, who probably didn't weigh more than sixty pounds, sat on the mud floor, cradling a baby in her lap. Another of her children had died the day before. She was blank with grief. Furtado asked: How could a wealthy nation like ours not share some of our bounty with this starving mother?

Hunger is inexcusable, especially because it is curable, and the United States can make a major difference while simultaneously helping to sustain our farmers. But there's also a push by the U.S. government and organizations like former United Nations secretary-general Kofi Annan's Alliance for a Green Revolution in Africa to help farmers overseas gain access to better seeds and soil to improve their crop production, an effective way to reduce poverty and hunger and increase economic growth.

We may not be able to deliver good medical care to the world's population (although the Bill & Melinda Gates Foundation is trying to do that, along with their international work to help farmers). But with a reasonable effort we can eliminate hunger. We have a surplus of food to feed everyone, computers to track food production and movement, machines to pick the harvest, and faster, more efficient transportation. We have better seeds and methods of growing them.

And all these years later, I still believe that food aid advances peace. Take any family with little kids: if lunch or dinner is delayed too long, they start scrapping with each other. It puts them on edge.

It's exactly the same on an international scale. An undernourished populace can never be stable, self-confident, or creative. You're more likely to get severe tensions and conflict in a society that doesn't know where their next meal is to be found.

One of the most ingenious programs I've heard about in years—the Global Alliance for Clean Cookstoves—came out of Hillary Rodham Clinton's State Department in 2010. It turns out that when aid agencies provide food to refugees and other people in conflict zones, women still have to search for scarce fuel to cook with, risking brutalization, rape, and other violent attacks. Using clean fuel and efficient stoves minimizes these perils. And it's hard to believe that in the second decade of the twenty-first century, three billion people still cook their meals on crude stoves or over open fires with solid fuels such as wood, dung, and charcoal. The smoke exposure alone kills nearly two million women and children each year. Now the public-private Alliance is giving stoves—some portable, others built directly into people's homes—to communities across Asia, sub-Saharan Africa, and Latin America.

How fortunate we are in the United States that preparing a simple dinner does not come with the same high risks. And yet, here at home, "foraging" for food involves an entirely different set of problems. Some 23.5 million people live in "food deserts"—poor or rural areas with a relative abundance of fast-food restaurants and convenience stores but no supermarkets—and not an apple or a celery stick to be found. A cheeseburger, french fries, and a Coke can be a delicious meal, but day after day this high-fat, high-sodium, high-sugar combo does not make for a balanced diet. It can lead to obesity and, over the long term, diabetes, heart disease, and cancer, creating enormous future health care costs for our nation.

This is simply a problem we ought not to have in the wealthiest country in the world. In 2010, President Obama signed the Healthy Food Financing Initiative, giving $400 million in loans, grants, and tax credits to businesses that support solutions, ranging from building a new grocery store to putting refrigerated units in convenience stores and stocking them with fresh fruit. But House Republicans have tried to eliminate this program completely.

Obesity is not something we can afford to sidestep in this country. One in three children in the overall population is either overweight or obese, and the numbers are higher for African American and Hispanic children. First Lady Michelle Obama has set the goal of fixing this untenable health problem within a generation, and I'm certainly hoping her signature program, Let's Move!, is successful. The Obama administration made an extraordinary deal with Walmart, the nation's largest retailer, to lower the fat, salt, and sugar content in the foods it sells over the next few years.

Any program like this is about creating awareness, and Mrs. Obama has made quite a stir. She's planted a vegetable garden at the White House, and she goes around the country doing workouts with schoolchildren and talking to them about eating fresh vegetables. Nutrition education is a problem we tried to address on the Senate select committee when we issued the first dietary recommendations to the public and, for the first time, explained the link between diet and disease. We want people to get enough food so they aren't hungry, but we need to teach them about the right kinds and amounts to eat to stay healthy.

I am sincerely hoping that the rancor between Democrats and Republicans in Washington subsides and that we'll get back to breaking bread together. But the real point is that the internecine politics playing out in Washington is such small potatoes compared to the greater problem of nourishing our global citizens. In our modern world, it is unconscionable to let one single person suffer over food, whether from eating too little or, eventually, from eating too much of the wrong food. One battle we can win in America is the battle against both hunger and obesity. Few challenges can provide a sweeter, more gratifying victory at so little cost.

IMMIGRATION

If you live in the United States but are not Native American, you are here because you or your forebears came as immigrants—though not always voluntarily. My grandfather, Thomas McGovern, emigrated from Ireland in the first half of the nineteenth century, before the American Civil War, in which he fought as a member of the Union's Seventh Cavalry. A miner, he left his home in county Clare and struck out for coal-rich western Pennsylvania with his wife before eventually moving to Illinois and finally to Iowa.

My mother, Frances McLean, an Ontario, Canada, native, came to Aberdeen, South Dakota, from

Calgary to visit her sister, Margaret, who was keeping house for two bachelor uncles. Mother was working as a secretary when she met my preacher father, Joseph, sent by the Wesleyan Methodist church.

Like my family, most immigrants arrive with the desire to work hard, a dedication to our American ideals, a determination to succeed, and an eagerness to join in this great experiment of ours. These are qualities that make our country unique. We take pride in our melting-pot roots. Our diversity has been our strength. As historian Oscar Handlin put it, America is a "nation of immigrants."

But the vision of an open-armed welcome is a memory tempered by time. Ironically, and to our shame, a good many of us—assimilated immigrants and their children and grandchildren—have historically opposed admitting those who would come after.

Today we welcome some immigrants, particularly those with the specialized skills that we need to bolster high-tech and other industries. But we are locked into a polarizing national debate over the fate of the more than 11 million undocumented immigrants who crossed our borders illegally or overstayed their visas. In the Facebook and Twitter era we inhabit, it's easy to ratchet up anti-immigrant sentiment. Just as Father Charles Coughlin used his popular radio show in the 1930s to denounce President Roosevelt and stir anti-Semitism, today unfounded pass-along e-mails, right-wing websites loaded with false figures, and conservative politicians shouting outright untruths have attracted the fearful, not to mention donations.

Republicans mean to incite anger and fear as political weapons. As Democrats, we are compelled to stand up for our nation's newest residents and to clarify the record.

It's interesting to me that throughout history the argument against accepting immigrants has remained consistent. It did not matter where the newcomers originate, which language they speak, or which religion they follow; there have always been naysayers motivated by fear—fear of being displaced, fear of job loss, fear that our federal coffers would be emptied to provide the incoming with welfare checks, food stamps, housing, medical bills, and education for their children.

Contrary to reports on ultraconservative talk-radio programs, here are the facts: illegal immigrants cannot receive welfare, food stamps, housing assistance, Medicaid, or Medicare for hospitalizations. In fact, to receive Medicare, the applicant must show proof of American citizenship. Undocumented workers are eligible for only two public services: public school from kindergarten through high school for their children and emergency medical care. The law says that emergency rooms cannot turn away any person needing emergency treatment. But this mandate does not extend to life-threatening non-emergencies such as cancer treatments.

Also conveniently overlooked on the talk-show circuit: 8 million of the 11 to 12 million illegal immigrants in the United States pay Medicare, Social Security, and personal income taxes.

Finally, the only way an undocumented worker can get steady employment is to use a false Social Security number. The hiring company automatically deducts Medicaid and Social Security, as it does for all employees. But if the number is fake, the worker will never be able to claim benefits. According to the Social Security Administration, this unclaimed money—kept separately—makes up one-tenth of the Social Security surplus, and it is increasing by about $50 billion a year.

Some conservatives charge that many illegal immigrants in America were criminals in their own country or that they arrive as criminals, having broken the law by crossing the border.

They are lobbying for a punitive approach. Deport them. Refuse them drivers' licenses. Turn them away from emergency rooms in public hospitals. Toss their children—even those born in the United States and therefore American citizens—out of public schools.

A number of state legislatures have passed laws designed to push the undocumented out. In 2011, Alabama made it a crime to rent an apartment to an undocumented immigrant or give them a ride or other means of transportation. The state also requires public schools to determine the immigration status of all students and to report the cost of educating the children whose parents are in the United States illegally. Nor can the undocumented attend public colleges or universities.

Both Alabama and Arizona allow police officers to ask anyone they stop about their immigration status if they have a "reasonable suspicion." (It is unclear whether these statutes will ultimately be upheld by the federal courts.)

To my mind these actions are un-American. We are the country founded on the belief that all men are created equal, as Thomas Jefferson famously wrote in the Declaration of Independence, and where any boy or girl born here can grow up to run for president, as I did in 1972. It is flat-out wrong to refuse an education to an innocent child or medical care to a man having a heart attack. Democrats do not torment people because they are not the same nationality as we are. We stand up for them.

In fact, immigrants, like many Americans, have

given up all that is familiar and comforting in hopes of escaping poverty or oppression, improving their lives and their children's futures, and helping their relatives back home. It is the same dream that gave all non–Native Americans the nerve and pluck to leave their homelands for an unknown place.

They did not come easily or on a whim. Some walked hundreds of miles, only to be turned back at the border. They tried again—and again. Some paid smugglers, forded rivers, and crossed deserts while crammed into hot, airless trucks. Like the immigrants before them, they have sacrificed to get here and lived in the shadows to stay. Many have been here for years, even decades, and have done grueling labor for meager wages, and most continue to work at low-wage jobs while living in substandard housing, sometimes paying premium rent to buy an unscrupulous landlord's silence. They have cleaned our houses, picked our crops, dug our ditches, slaughtered our livestock. They have had children here, put their children in school here, and paid taxes here. They have participated in our communities, joined churches, and volunteered. Some have joined the military and served in war zones.

If we are honest with ourselves, we know that in the days before computers and background checks, some of our forefathers entered the United States illegally. In fact, some of our earliest legal settlers were convicts sent by England to the colonies—an estimated 50,000 between 1620 and the start of the American Revolution in 1775. Obviously, I am not advocating importing hardened criminals. I am simply saying that much of our own past is imperfect— beginning at the beginning.

Nor was the land that we seek to keep immigrants out of ours to take. The Black Hills of South Dakota, in my home state, witnessed how white men— that period's immigrants—treated Native Americans, stealing their land and, in many cases, their lives. A monument, incomplete after more than six decades, memorializes the Native Americans who battled bravely but ultimately in vain to hold on to their expansive territory and their way of life. Unlike

Mount Rushmore, into which the likenesses of George Washington, Thomas Jefferson, Abraham Lincoln, and Theodore Roosevelt have been carved, the Crazy Horse Memorial is formed from an entire mountain. Begun in 1948, the world's largest sculpture is a tribute to the Lakota warrior who for years fought federal encroachment, most famously in the Battle of the Little Bighorn in 1876. Under Crazy Horse's command, Sioux Indians famously trapped and killed Lieutenant Colonel George Armstrong Custer and his men. The Indians won the battle, but within a year the federal government had its retribution. The United States had given the Black Hills to the Indians in a treaty in 1868. Afterward, gold was discovered, and prospectors poured in. Following Custer's defeat, our government took the land back. The brilliant, rough-cut sculptor Korczak Ziolkowski launched and shaped the huge Crazy Horse monument as a tribute to the Indians. Following his death, Ziolkowski's remarkable widow, Ruth, and children have kept the project moving forward.

Our treatment of North America's inhabitants

is among the most shameful parts of our history. And that continues. Today, Native Americans have lower education and income levels and higher unemployment and poverty rates than the population as a whole. Their infant death rate is 40 percent higher than it is among white Americans. Native Americans have higher instances of diabetes, cancer, AIDS, strokes, substance abuse, and suicide.

I am saddened by my personal failure, as a U.S. senator, to do more to help Native Americans in my state and others. I wish I had given more time and energy to their cause. I wish I had worked harder to be their voice in Washington.

I cannot right those regrets. We can't undo the awful way African Americans and Native Americans were treated in days gone by. We can't un-shun the millions of immigrants who felt the sting of being unwanted when signs such as "No Irish Need Apply" hung on employers' doors.

But as Democrats we must carry these critical lessons forward. We can do what's right by the millions of people who long to become Americans today.

Immigrants did not come here to break our laws. They came to live our dream.

They, like us, are part of the fabric of this nation. We must give them the opportunity to fully participate in American life, free from worry that they will be discovered and sent back to a place that no longer is their home. We need to give them a path to citizenship.

We should require illegal immigrants to come forward, pay a penalty, pay taxes, obtain work permits, and pass criminal background checks. After living legally in the United States for a set number of years and satisfying all requirements, they could apply to become American citizens.

Meanwhile, we can update our immigration laws. We need a sensible way to control immigration. We can, for instance, give preference to immigrants who have family members in the United States and to those who have skills that meet our economic needs. I believe that if someone comes from another country to attend a university in the United States, they should have a chance to stay here, to use the skills that they learn here to better our economy.

Similarly, Congress should pass the Development, Relief and Education for Alien Minors Act, known more simply as the DREAM Act, which would provide a path to citizenship for young people who came to the United States illegally when they were children and who enroll in an American college or university or choose to serve in our military. Democrats have supported this bill, but Republicans have blocked it from becoming law. It's bad enough that we would prevent adults who are undocumented from reaching their full potential in this country, but to penalize young people is counterproductive and absurd. Let's not create a permanent multigenerational underclass. Let's create a generation of high achievers who can bring us innovation, start businesses, stimulate employment, and contribute to the general welfare.

That is good business.

Currently, employers take advantage of undocumented immigrants. They pay them low wages and force them to work long hours, often under very poor conditions. They get away with it because workers are afraid to speak out. This unethical behavior suppresses wages for everyone. If employers have to pay a decent wage to those at the lowest rungs of the economic ladder, they will have to pay more for those on each successive rung. Everyone benefits.

Our country was built on the aspirations and talents of people who came here from other places. We are stronger—our *economy* is stronger—because of them. They bring new ideas—new ways of doing things—that enhance us all. According to the Partnership for a New American Economy, a bipartisan organization of business leaders and mayors, more than 40 percent of the 2010 Fortune 500 companies were founded by immigrants or their children. Those companies employ more than 10 million people worldwide and have combined revenues of $4.2 trillion—more than the gross domestic product of every nation in the world save the United States, China, and Japan. Imagine where we would be without those immigrant entrepreneurs.

Or—and here I'm speaking as both a Democrat and as a lifelong St. Louis Cardinals fan—without Albert Pujols, who, among his other distinctions, in

2010, led baseball players in both the National and American Leagues in batting, slugging, and on-base percentage. Pujols, who hails from the Dominican Republic, isn't taking anyone else's job. He and other players from Japan, South Korea, Cuba, Mexico, Nicaragua, Colombia, and Venezuela—immigrants all—are adding to the general goodwill of our nation's entertainment. It's easy to acknowledge their contribution when they have recognizable faces and the distinction of having been Rookie of the Year or their league's Most Valuable Player noted beside their names in the record books. The trick for us Democrats is to stand up for the millions of immigrants who have none of these things going for them.

EDUCATION

In the spring of my junior year at Mitchell High School, my American history teacher, Bob Pearson, doglegged from that day's lesson to tell us his philosophy on life. Pearson had already earned my devotion as the school's debate coach. Years earlier, as a first-grader, I suffered from such painful shyness that I refused to read aloud or even recite or answer a question in class. My lack of participation was so pronounced that at the end of the year my teacher passed me only "on condition."

I overcame some of my reticence between second grade and high school. But I owe the real change in my personality to Pearson, whom my sophomore English literature teacher, Rose Hopfner, encouraged me to meet. Pearson taught me to speak without notes and to deliver my points logically and forcefully. Under his guidance I was transformed from a stammering teenager into a confident young man, able to articulate my views on a growing number of public issues. (In college, at Dakota Wesleyan University, I became a champion debater with the help of a colleague, Matthew Smith Jr.)

In his spontaneous lecture that day, Pearson told us that life's highest goal is service to others and that imagination is the key to a useful and satisfying career.

Over the years my imagination expanded to take me many unexpected places: I never dreamed then that I would become a U.S. congressman, senator, presidential nominee, or ambassador. But first, because of Bob Pearson's positive influence, I decided to become a history professor. And thanks to the GI Bill, established in 1944 for my generation of veterans returning home from World War II, I was able to accomplish my goal, earning a Ph.D. in history at Northwestern University in 1953.

When I think back on it, with the exception of the two and a half years I was enrolled at the private Dakota Wesleyan University, I owe my education to the federal government. My elementary and secondary-school education was paid for by our town and state. When I was a U.S. senator living with my family in suburban Maryland, just outside Washington, D.C., my wife, Eleanor, and I chose to put our children through the local public schools (with short-term exceptions for two of our daughters). I believed in the egalitarian aspect of public schools, the fact that kids get to mingle with all sorts of Americans—and I still do. Learning alongside and sitting down to lunch with people who may be different helps form the basis for compassion, which is essential to being a Democrat.

Yes, I'm sure that some private academies offer students more one-on-one attention and perhaps more intellectual stimulation than the neighborhood public school. But that doesn't change my strongly held view that public funds should be invested in public education. Especially now, with a growing array of public charter schools, parents have more choice than ever if they don't like what they see at the traditional school down the street. But voucher programs that use public money to send kids to private school only divert money away from the overall goal of making U.S. public schools as robust as possible.

How do we get our schools to be the best they can be? While Democrats recognize that education is a local issue, we are also certain that it is a national one. I can think of no more valuable contribution that the government (city, state, and federal) makes to our citizens—with the possible exception of health care. I was aghast a couple of years ago when I heard that, to save money, Hawaii's Republican governor decided to furlough for seventeen Fridays a year not just teachers—a disturbing practice in itself—but also the state's 171,000 students, including children at the same elementary school once attended by President Barack Obama.

The controversial cutback lasted a year before it

was discontinued. But the very notion that anyone thought this was okay—that furloughing students was fair game—violated an essential Democratic principle: educating our children is sacrosanct. That's why, when I served on the House Committee on Education and Labor as a freshman congressman, and throughout my years in the Senate, I supported any program that I felt would strengthen our nation's elementary, secondary, or higher education.

Republicans are fickle about the federal government's role in education. From time to time, including in 1980, when Ronald Reagan was campaigning for his first term as president, various GOP leaders have talked of shuttering the Department of Education altogether, arguing that federal funding for schools is ineffective and that only states and communities should shape our school systems.

So it was a big deal in 2001 when President George W. Bush and my close friend Ted Kennedy managed to win bipartisan support for the No Child Left Behind Act (NCLB)—and I would excuse them if they thought the hard part was over.

But the truth is that the main law guiding our kindergarten-through-twelfth-grade education has been something of a headache—for both parties—since the day it was signed.

NCLB's main thrust is about accountability for students and teachers. But I'm not surprised at the complaints by millions of parents that NCLB raises the standards for the children at the bottom while ignoring the needs of our high-achieving children at the top. Another criticism: by focusing the tests on reading and math, other vital subjects like social studies, science, art, music, and physical education are given shorter shrift (although at the high school level this is completely untrue). And I understand the hostility of teachers and administrators, who have experienced the law as a series of threats and punishments.

The real positives I see are those that Kennedy himself highlighted in a 2008 op-ed piece he published in the *Washington Post*. We can no longer hide behind the achievements of our best-performing students. Instead, as he wrote, "the law demands that all children must benefit—black or white, immigrant or native-born, rich or poor, disabled or not. . . . Across the country, schools are poring over student data to identify weaknesses in instruction and to improve teaching and learning." Students in these groups have demonstrated achievement in both math and reading—although the National Assessment of Educational Progress (NAEP), also known as "the nation's report card," shows that we still have a great deal more work to do in closing the gaps between white students and others.

Looking back on the No Child Left Behind Act's turbulent decade, I would say its impact on K–12 education has been mixed. Not quite three-fourths of America's students graduate from high school, and of those who go to college, a third require remedial courses. But from my years in Congress, I know firsthand how difficult it can be to perfect legislation the first time. We owe it to our students, their parents, our teachers, and our principals not to scrap it but to fix it. This will require persistence—one of the very values we try to instill in our children—and that may be tough in this polarized political climate. Since the

2008 election, the bipartisan coalition has begun to unravel as some conservatives on Capitol Hill rediscover their fundamental commitment to states' rights and their distaste for federal intrusion into education-related matters. This couldn't come at a worse time. In 2011 Republican governor Scott Walker of Wisconsin cut $800 million out of his state's education budget. Combined with a reduction in school district property tax authority, the Badger State—whose motto, ironically, is "Forward"—is spending an average of $1,449 less per pupil a year for the next two years. There aren't enough school bake sales in the universe to make up this difference!

I also think that, while important, accountability rooted in standardized testing is just a start when it comes to thinking about our schools and educators. My heroes at Mitchell High, Bob Pearson and Rose Hopfner, loved their jobs—you could tell by the way they handled themselves around us. Our slightest progress elicited their praise. You could even say that they nursed me into running for Congress; I know I would never have had the nerve to put myself on such a public stage without their early encouragement. I say all this even though Bob Pearson was a devoted Republican. After all, the Republicans need all the good people they can recruit. My friend and Senate colleague Gene McCarthy, a skilled man with a sharp wit, once observed: "The Republicans have a lot of good Republicans. They just never run any of them for office."

But times are a good bit more complicated now than they were when I was in high school, and a solid education rests on so much more than educators' enthusiasm—or even on their quality. We must provide ongoing teacher training and mentoring and the necessary resources not just to improve the job instructors do in class but their capacity to deal with out-of-school factors that some children bring into the classroom as surely as they carry a backpack. These include poverty, a history of family and neighborhood violence, poor health, and a lack of parental know-how and involvement. We need to connect our students with social workers and counselors when necessary. We need to invest in school buildings, books, and materials. We need to make sure that no child skips breakfast or lunch because he or she cannot afford to pay. This last point is of particular importance to me as it was in 1970, when Bob Dole and I established both the reduced-price and free lunch program and a free breakfast program that continues today.

My other frustration with No Child Left Behind has to do with the tumult that surrounds it. Since the beginning, it has consumed such vast amounts of energy and attention that policy makers have had neither the time nor the resources to devote to the two other issues that should be near the top of our education policy agenda: access to early childhood programs and college affordability.

The Democratic Party's commitment to the well-being of young children is and always has been one of our most important and ennobling missions. Our dedication has been made manifest through legislation such as Head Start and Women, Infants, and Children (WIC), the nutrition program for pregnant women and their children. Whatever our interest in kindergarten-through-twelfth-grade education, we must continue to insist, without apology, that we have no higher priority than to protect the welfare of those who are too young to protect themselves. That's both a moral argument and an economic one. Studies by Nobel Prize–winning economist James Heckman of the University of Chicago show that investments in early childhood and preschool programs generate far greater returns to the economy at large than do comparable investments in K–12 education or job training programs. Giving children a firm foundation between birth and the age of five, when their brains are developing most rapidly, lowers deficits, reducing both the later need for expensive special education and grade retention. Taking children in hand before kindergarten makes it less likely they will become juvenile delinquents, less likely they will get pregnant as teenagers, and more likely they will graduate from high school than those who we don't attend to early on.

James Heckman said that "the accident of birth is the greatest source of inequality," adding that higher standards, smaller classrooms, and more Internet access—all things that our policy makers have pushed in kindergarten through twelfth grade—"have less impact than we think." What does matter is giving preschoolers the keystone cognitive skills like pre-reading and pre-math and character skills like perseverance, self-control, and getting along with others that are crucial to success at every stage of life. Imagine that at three years old a low-income child, whose parents are less likely to stress language development, read to them, and play word games, has been exposed to 30 million fewer words than a child of middle-class parents. These children are behind even before they learn how to sound out their ABCs.

And once they're behind, research shows, they tend to stay there.

As Democrats, we need to stop apologizing for Head Start. Instead, let's improve it, expand it, and treasure it for what it is: a helping hand for our neediest children. We need to offer high-quality public preschool to all children whose parents want to send them. And we must expand and fully fund proven initiatives such as the Nurse-Family Partnership program and WIC.

But we cannot just stop at our youngest learners; we must look at ways to make post-secondary education more affordable. For most Americans, paying for college is the largest single purchase families make besides our homes. Over the past twenty years, rising college costs have outpaced that of health care, food, and energy. In their book *Higher Education? How Colleges Are Wasting Our Money and Failing Our Kids—and What We Can Do About It*, Andrew Hacker and Claudia Dreifus note that "for every $1,000 parents were asked to pay in 1982, they must hand over $2,540 in real money today." The increase at traditionally affordable public universities has been even steeper.

According to the College Board, in-state tuition and fees at a public four-year institution in 2010–11 averaged $7,605, out-of-state tuition and fees averaged $11,990, and four-year liberal arts colleges averaged $27,293. Add room and board, books and supplies, trips home, and the occasional purchase of a school sweatshirt, and the prices rise to $20,339, $24,724, and $40,027, respectively. And that's just for one year!

The money has gone to pay college presidents (now being given executive compensation packages on a par with any well-paid corporate CEO), tenured faculty, an expanded army of administrators, and amenities—en suite dormitories, gyms, Jacuzzis, food courts—that make students clamor to go there. Hacker and Dreifus also point out that another reason colleges are more expensive today is a bit of marketing: people think they get what they pay for.

It's little wonder that 60 percent of our students walk away on graduation day not just with a diploma but also with debt that stacks their work life against them from the beginning. In 2009, according to the Project on Student Debt, 67 percent of students finished four years of college carrying an average of $24,000 in loans. Among students graduating from for-profit universities, the numbers are typically much higher. And this is just the start. I recently read of one young woman studying to become a veterinarian who owes a half million dollars in tuition fees—and she hasn't examined her first cat. Even middle-class families who have saved diligently would buckle under that burden. My own children worry all the time about how they will pay for college for their children and grandchildren.

Democrats are usually portrayed as the party of fiscal irresponsibility, but often we are the watchdogs guarding ordinary Americans' checkbooks against corporate predators. President Obama and congressional Democrats have reined in abusive credit card companies, voracious mortgage bankers, and for-profit companies offering loans to naive high school students and their financially strapped parents. Bill Clinton signed the first direct loan program into law as one of his earliest acts as president in 1993, a program that Barack Obama extended under the Health Care and Education Reconciliation Act of 2010. Now, rather than banks, all new college loans will go through the Department of Education. The law also lowered the repayment cap for new borrowers from 15 percent to 10 percent and decreased the life span of a college loan from twenty-five years to twenty years.

This is all good.

But the main problem, especially in this tough economy, is that the price tag on college is high enough to dissuade many young adults and their parents from even considering the option. It is time for Democrats to end this downward spiraling chapter in American higher education. Today, just over 40 percent of U.S. adults between the ages of twenty-five and sixty-four have a two-year college degree or better, putting us sixth—between New Zealand and Finland—among the thirty-six countries included in the Organisation for Economic Co-operation and Development's most recent rankings. Significantly, while our college attainment rate stays stagnant, other industrialized countries are passing us by.

Although I pride myself in being forward-thinking, this is one case where I believe the solution lies in an earlier time: let's make the equivalent of the GI Bill available to *all* lower- and middle-income Americans who have successfully completed high school to cover high-quality community college, college, and professional or graduate school education. This universal higher-education allowance is similar to what many countries in Europe do, where qualified college students not only attend for free but even receive a grant to help defray living expenses. The downside, of course, is that in Germany, less than a third of young people attend university, where admission is based solely on exam results.

A vigorous debate has arisen recently over whether or not everyone needs to go to college. I don't understand why this is even up for discussion. Do these same people think we should turn back the clock one hundred years, before there was universal high school too—or put children right to work like my father, who toiled long days in a coal mine as a boy? College was a part of the American Dream even before the colonies won their independence. Nine colleges and universities were established on our shores before

1776. Good Democrats want for everyone what we want for ourselves. And who among us doesn't count on sending our children to college?

A well-rounded, civilized, and functioning society needs people who can repair our cars, roofs, appliances, toilets, computers, elevators, and streetlights—and these jobs can be done without a college degree. But research by Anthony Carnevale at the Georgetown University Center on Education and the Workforce indicates that even for those jobs that don't require a bachelor's degree, a college education still translates into a higher salary. And what if one day these plumbers and technicians want to establish a wind farm or design a new electric car? A college education will give them the needed flexibility to make a change in our increasingly mobile society.

Well-paying low-skill jobs that were once the hallmark of American industry are disappearing rapidly. In an increasingly globalized economy where capital and technology are fluid, it is important to be as competitive as possible. There's a reason that President Obama has called for increasing the share of Americans who go to college. It's not because he wants one for the record books. It's because it's good for the nation.

The gap between college-educated haves and un-educated have-nots continues to grow wider, according to another Center on Education and the Workforce study. In 1963, when I was a freshman senator, a typical college graduate earned 1.4 times the hourly rate of a high school graduate. By 2009 that number had nearly doubled, even without including health insurance and pension plans. And while our nation's overall unemployment rate is 9.1 percent, college graduates have fared twice as well, with just 4.5 percent out of work.

I am not an economist, but I know this much: part of the nation's growth after World War II was fueled by the increased taxes paid by better-educated veterans who found work at better pay scales than previous generations. Receiving an education they would not have otherwise gotten enabled many Americans to get a foothold in the middle class. Dollar for dollar it may be the greatest educational success story in

American history. And I guarantee this expense will have a bigger payoff than our endless spending on military matters, including the senseless wars in Iraq and Afghanistan.

We are struggling to pay for two wars, while a third conflict in Libya pulled us in too. At home, we debate how to become more competitive in the world. But even when a school must leave its science teacher slots unfilled for budgetary reasons, we fail to connect these dots. This is not a case of too few resources, it's a case of misplaced national priorities, and we Democrats need to hammer this point home.

During World War II, when the weather was bad and we couldn't fly our bombing missions, I would stretch across the cot in my tent in Cerignola, Italy, and read. One book I spent a lot of time on was Charles and Mary Beard's two-thousand-page *The Rise of American Civilization*, which looked beyond our military and diplomatic achievements to the many elements that formed our nascent society. The authors included a quotation by Voltaire in the preface that I underlined: "I wish to write a history, not of wars, but of society . . . I want to know what were the steps by which mankind passed from barbarism to civilization."

Each June, we engage in a national ritual of gathering our college graduates on manicured lawns, hand them their diplomas, and give commencement addresses daring them to greatness. But what is left unsaid—what we Democrats must fix if we are ever to have a truly civilized society—is that there is no greatness to be had until we fix the inequalities in our education system.

Fellow Democrats, never forget that it was FDR—a man of wealth with degrees from Groton, Harvard, and Columbia—who put the needs of the country ahead of his own economic interests. Republicans labeled him a traitor to his class.

PUTTING AMERICA
BACK TO WORK

I got my first job at the age of fourteen, thanks to the natural tendency of grass to grow and the energy that comes with youth. One of our Mitchell, South Dakota, neighbors, Mrs. Truax, hired me to mow and edge her lawn and trim the front hedge. Mrs. Truax was a charming woman who demanded attention to detail. I must have met her standards, because by the end of the summer I got a 50 percent raise, leaping from ten to fifteen cents an hour. The next summer I developed a thriving business, commanding twenty-five cents an hour to weed gardens and cut grass for a dozen families around town. I don't remember my parents ever giving me pocket money after I started high school.

My yard business taught me what the next seven decades of my life confirmed: there is no substitute for a good day's work. A job puts food on a family's table and shoes on their feet, pays mortgages and medical bills, and engages the mind and/or the body. It builds a sense of self-worth that is essential to one's well-being. Even at my advanced age, I know I would be frustrated if I weren't absorbed in various projects. Retirement for me has meant reducing my workdays from fourteen hours to twelve!

Contrast these pluses with the nearly 14 million jobless Americans (adding the two million more who are unemployed but have stopped applying for work), and one can begin to get a sense of the profound loss in earnings, opportunities, ego, and spirit that Americans have suffered since 2007, when the housing bubble burst and ushered in the Great Recession. These are difficult times.

No good Democrat wants our neighbors sitting at home, unable to earn an income by their own sweat or ingenuity. This is such a basic tenet that I would challenge anyone to disagree. The opportunity to make a living is the very foundation of America, no matter what political party one affiliates with.

But the stark fact, according to a report by the California Budget Project, is that there are four times as many people job hunting as there are positions to fill. The longer you're unemployed, the less likely you are to get hired. It angers me that people eager to work are often treated no better than a carton of milk—as if they have a shelf life. Finding work is harder today because—besides our overall economic slowdown—millions of jobs have been shipped overseas, where labor is cheaper. It's little wonder that in recent surveys a majority of Americans say they are feeling pessimistic about the future.

As a seven-year-old at the start of the Great Depression, I remember seeing the stricken faces of the bankers, store owners, and farmers who had lost their incomes and their property to bankruptcy and foreclosure. It was confusing to see grown-ups— who were in my mind all-powerful—unable to rescue themselves and their families. My father, a Wesleyan Methodist minister, was lucky: as long as God was in business, he stayed employed. The majority of women, including my mother, were homemakers, perhaps an even more exhausting job in those days before appliances. But suddenly fathers, the providers, were home too.

The Democratic Party I fell hard for did not tolerate unemployment. When Franklin Roosevelt took the oath of office in March 1933, he looked out on a national landscape in far worse shape than ours is now. FDR seized on the most powerful tool at his disposal—the federal government—to get the stalled economy moving. His largest and best-known solution was to create the Works Progress Administration, which, between 1935 and 1943, hired eight and half million people to build or improve our country's public works.

The WPA is a prime example of win-win. People got steady paychecks that fed families, the nation's economic engine, and the national hope that better days were coming. The United States got needed roads and airfields. Nearly every community boasted a new park, bridge, or school. The number of rural homes with electricity doubled. In my hometown, we got a beautiful new courthouse that we are still using with pride.

In true Democratic fashion, the WPA also acknowledged the value of the arts, hiring hundreds of actors, writers, painters, photographers, and historians. I've read that these creative types didn't always appreciate having to clock into their government job at nine a.m. Nonetheless they produced some of our country's most enduring works—murals in libraries and post offices, local histories and travel guides, and photographs that brought the destruction of the Depression home to the nation. *Migrant Mother*, Dorothea Lange's 1936 photo of a woman at a California pea pickers' camp, worry creasing her face, became the iconic image of the era.

In 2009, seventy-six years after Roosevelt entered the White House, our new president, Barack Obama, had barely changed out of his inaugural tuxedo before he got down to work the next day, pushing

Congress for a stimulus bill to staunch the worst effects of the recession. I thought his first major piece of legislation, the $787 million American Recovery and Reinvestment Act, was the right approach. It helped keep teachers in classrooms, established electronic health care records, invested in green technology, and repaired roads and bridges, among many other initiatives. All told, it saved or created about three million jobs. It may have prevented the recession from becoming a depression; I only wish it had been even larger than it was—not smaller, as the act's opponents advocated.

But it didn't take long for some conservatives and libertarians to decide that spending money to stem unemployment had hampered, not helped, our economy. To them, federal debt was more important than putting Americans back to work. And with that, the Tea Party movement was born.

I don't mean to be rude, but I do mean to be blunt: no one—conservative or liberal—is cheering the increased debt load. But had we not borrowed, our nation's economy would have continued to careen downhill. The stimulus helped stabilize the country and lay the groundwork for a recovery, however fragile.

The problem, as I mentioned, is that the stimulus wasn't large enough to yield a far-reaching, long-term effect. Now that the money has been spent, local governments have begun to shed jobs—so far, nearly a half million since their 2008 peak. In school districts across the country, superintendents have discarded extracurricular activities, cut back on classroom supplies, dismissed administrative staff, and frozen salaries. When that wasn't enough, many schools had to fire their librarians to stave off even more difficult cuts, such as discontinuing full-day kindergarten. The end is not yet in sight.

Nor have states been exempt. The governors of New Jersey and Wisconsin have used their local budget crunches as an excuse to break up public sector labor unions. We Democrats ought to know better. We cannot expect our firefighters and police officers to put themselves in harm's way for us and then steal their economic security.

As a South Dakotan, I am as thrifty as anyone I know. It is how my parents reared me. But had Congress been able to agree on a larger stimulus, my bet is that we would not be losing jobs now. And the problem, besides the soul-sapping aspects of being laid off, is that each person collecting unemployment means fewer dollars recycled back into the economy.

For all of the GOP's faith in supply-side economics—lowering taxes to spur the economy by producing more goods and services (the approach popularized by Ronald Reagan and carried forth by George W. Bush)—the idea isn't worth a hoot in a rain barrel. This Republican policy helped the wealthiest Americans squirrel away the money they saved in income taxes and capital gains taxes to become even wealthier. In 2007, the top 1 percent of U.S. households received tax cuts averaging $41,077, which lifted their after-tax incomes by 5.0 percent, according to the Urban-Brookings Tax Policy Center. And within the top 1 percent, households with incomes over $1 million received tax cuts averaging $114,000, resulting in an after-tax income jump of 5.7 percent.

But the so-called trickle-down effect that supply-siders count on to create jobs never materialized.

It is past time for the supply-side myth to be replaced by something that works: demand-side economics. As in Franklin Roosevelt's day, our party should push to supplement private employment with public efforts to expand the workforce—to spark consumer demand by putting money in people's pockets. Unlike the wealthy, when the poor and middle class earn more, the money goes right back into the economy, spent on food, clothes, transportation, and other necessities. Greater demand causes the local grocery store chain to add another cashier, or the local Walmart another greeter. And with each new hire, the positive cycle begins again.

I am all for balancing the budget, but first things first: we need to think innovatively and broadly about creating new jobs, following the WPA model. We ought to use American talent and tax money to create lasting improvements.

Let's start with one of President Obama's pet projects: building the world's best high-speed railway

to serve 80 percent of the country by 2025. Conservatives tend to disparage or even mock the plan as more
needless big government spending.

Here's why I believe they are wrong. President
Eisenhower, one of my heroes, initiated the Interstate
Highway System (IHS) more than a half century ago.
As the South Dakota State Democratic Party executive secretary in the mid-1950s, before the interstate
system was completed, I remember how long it took
me to drive from town to town on two-lane roads.

Today, freeways are such a part of American life
that we rarely think of them as more than the route
home for Thanksgiving. But the system the IHS built,
primarily to allow military convoys to cross the country efficiently, is still "the economic engine that drives
this country's prosperity," as *American History* mag-
azine noted. With the dawn of what is sometimes
called "Eisenhower's autobahn," American businesses
were able to instantly expand their territory and increase their bottom lines. During its first forty years
the Interstate spawned more than seven million jobs
and bumped up the nation's productivity by 25 per-

cent. Every dollar spent on highway construction generates six dollars in return. The existence of freeways has allowed millions of Americans to buy homes in the suburbs and commute to work.

Fast trains would do for the nation in the twenty-first century what the Interstate Highway System did in the twentieth. I have been advocating such a rail system for forty years. A study by the nonpartisan U.S. PIRG (the federation of state Public Interest Research Groups) shows that no matter how successful the IHS has been, money spent today on public transportation creates twice as many jobs as funds spent on highways. And the benefits would be immediate, since one in five of the nation's unemployed is a laid-off construction worker. Shuttered plants could be retrofitted to build and maintain new locomotives and cars, creating manufacturing jobs. Engineers would be needed to grade new routes. We would require conductors, operators, ticket takers, and repair people. The ripples would spread far and wide.

China, Japan, and Europe have long relied on bullet trains that run at 200 miles per hour, while the United States merely chugs along behind them. Contrast the top speed for most U.S. trains—regular passenger trains run at 59 miles per hour—with high-speed trains (defined as anything above 160 miles per hour) on new track. Such an interconnected system would dramatically reduce traffic congestion, decrease the number of highway injuries and fatalities, and prolong the life spans of our roadways. Fewer drivers would mean cutting greenhouse gases and dialing back our dependence on gasoline. An easy commute would encourage suburban home buying, help stabilize home values, and lower the transportation costs for many. By spending fewer hours behind the wheel, commuters would be more productive—or even gain much-sought family or relaxation time.

I am baffled by the shortsightedness of the Republican governors of Florida, Ohio, and Wisconsin who turned away federal money their states had won for high-speed rail projects. Governor Rick Scott of Florida rejected $2.4 billion, which would have nearly paid for the nation's first bullet train between Orlando and Tampa. His fear was that the train would somehow become a costly "boondoggle." With it he returned approximately 20,000 temporary and permanent jobs for his constituents at a time when the state unemployment rate was 12.5 percent. He gave up a high-speed train that could, one day, be part of a coast-to-coast network—a train that could serve commuters and encourage tourists. As a part-time Florida resident, I have heard both Republican and Democratic Florida voters say that Scott will be a one-term governor. One can only hope.

A high-speed train network is admittedly a huge project. But there are also thousands of comparatively smaller, essential public works jobs that need tackling. The broken levees after Hurricane Katrina that resulted in the flooding of New Orleans in 2005; the bursting of the Kaloko Reservoir dam in Kauai, Hawaii, in 2006; and the rush-hour collapse of the Interstate 35W Bridge in downtown Minneapolis in 2007 are a few high-profile disasters that likely could have been prevented if we had properly cared for our nation's infrastructure. That's just the start. According to the U.S. Department of Transportation, a quarter of our 600,000 bridges need repairs, and our substandard roads are "a significant factor" in one-third of the 43,000 auto fatalities each year. Our power grids are struggling to keep up with increased energy demands. As Donald F. Kettl, dean of the School of Public Policy at the University of Maryland, put it, "Much of America is being held together with Scotch tape, baling wire, and prayers."

We have put these tasks off just as many homeowners do; maintenance is costly and unglamorous. There always seem to be more pressing needs. But of course delaying these long-overdue projects eventually costs us even more. Today, our fixer-upper of a country cannot operate at full capacity. This is the right moment to repair the metaphorical leaky roof and, in the process, give more out-of-work people a paycheck.

Besides outright job creation, there are other critical steps we ought to be taking to reduce the unemployment rolls. By some estimates, fully a quarter of our joblessness is due to structural unemployment, a mismatch between workers and openings. A 2010 report by the Hamilton Project and the Center for American Progress indicates that in this information age, many middle-class Americans possess outmoded skills. But that alone doesn't account for the misalignment. A 2009 National Association of Manufacturers survey indicated that a third of companies lacked qualified scientists and engineers. With the economy operating below capacity, now is the time to invest in job training programs and additional education to help workers retool. While many Democrats in Congress understand this, there aren't enough votes to save the U.S. Department of Labor's job training programs from the House Republicans' budget ax. But I believe this is a case where the government shouldn't have to bear the full burden. Journalist Robert Samuelson has urged American companies to be "a little bolder," to "make a small gamble that, by providing more training for workers, they might actually do themselves and the country some good." I agree. The past several decades have been marked by disloyalty on the part of companies and employees. It is high time to revive and strengthen the compact that traditionally bound business and workers.

Here are a few suggestions that would advance this cause: raising the minimum wage from $7.75 to $8.25 an hour would result in an almost instant payoff. The fifty-cent hourly increase would give some 10 million workers a raise, thereby flushing more money into the economy. Although naysayers argue that even a small bump in wages cuts into job creation, in fact the opposite is true, according to Heidi Shierholz, an economist with the nonpartisan Economic Policy Institute: an increase could generate 50,000 new jobs.

We must also expand on family-friendly labor policies. Conservatives are given to saying that the Democrats' idea of family-friendly is business-unfriendly. This propagates the false notion that Democrats are out to break small businesses.

Let me give you an example: when Bill Clinton signed the Family and Medical Leave Act into law in 1993, it was the first time mothers and fathers of a premature infant, people nursing a partner with cancer, or someone caring for a parent in last-stage dementia did not have to choose between shortchanging a loved one and holding on to the job that kept the family in food and health insurance. Employees can now take off twelve weeks to care for immediate family or for themselves, without pay, but with the promise that their job, or a similar position, will be available when they return. They retain benefits but pay their share. Small businesses are exempt, as the act applies only to employers with fifty or more workers living within seventy-five miles of their workplace. The cost to the employer is minimal. But for employees, already stretched and stressed, it is a blessing.

Nonetheless our work-family policies still lag far behind our industrialized counterparts. Between 1979 and 2006, the average American middle-class family's workweek lengthened by eleven hours. Think of all their children's soccer games American parents have missed! I wasn't around for a lot of my daughters' and son's growing-up years, and I regret it to this day. You do not get the time back.

America's work ethic is such that we toil longer hours than people in most other developed countries, including Japan, where, the Center for American Progress's Joan C. Williams and Heather Boushey note, "there's a word, karoshi, for 'death by overwork.'" At a minimum, most European Union countries set the workweek below forty hours and guarantee a certain number of fully subsidized sick days. Of the thirty nations in the Organisation for Economic Co-operation and Development, the United States alone does not guarantee paid maternity leave. And child care subsidies here, limited to the poor, are spotty at best. Given all these challenges, it's no wonder that, according to Williams and Boushey, 90 percent of American mothers and 95 percent of fathers say they experience work-family conflict.

In 1960, when I was a U.S. congressman, I was the breadwinner for our rollicking family of seven, and Eleanor stayed home to take care of our children, as 80 percent of mothers did. Today, this number has nearly flipped: 70 percent of American children live in homes where both parents work. Even so, salaries for lower- and middle-income Americans have not kept pace. The Economic Policy Institute reports that over the past thirty years, 34.6 percent of all U.S. income growth has gone to the top one-tenth of one percent of earners. In contrast, the bottom 90 percent of earners has seen only 15.9 percent growth. Think about that. The widening salary gap between U.S. CEOs and average workers is a demoralizing force. According to the AFL-CIO's Executive PayWatch, in 2010 the average chief executive of a Standard & Poor's Fortune 500 company earned $11.4 million. This eight-figure salary equals the paychecks of 28 U.S. presidents, 225 teachers, or 753 minimum-wage earners.

Another trend in the workplace is a significant drop in union membership, to the deafening applause of conservatives, who believe that unions drag our economy down. Today only 12 percent of American employees belong to a labor union, compared to about one-third between 1947 and 1973. But during those years, U.S. economic output tripled, growing at a rate of 3.8 percent a year, compared to 2.2 percent since 2001. And as membership has dropped, so has the share of income going to the American middle class.

With all these forces tugging people down, we don't have to look far to understand what keeps Americans awake a night. A recent Gallup "well-being" poll found that 40 percent of employed workers and 55 percent of underemployed workers said they were struggling or suffering.

Devaluing the hard work of the average person has become a systemic—and distressing—national problem. Preoccupied by job insecurity, stagnant salaries, and the need to care for their families in a hostile work environment, Americans cannot possibly focus on the greater good. You can't worry about clean air or water, better energy policies, or national education standards when you're wrapped up in gnawing questions over how to make a living, pay the mortgage, and afford this week's groceries.

As conscientious parents, we guide our children. We lay out the blueprint for success. We underscore our values until they are (we hope) absorbed. We tell them as our parents taught us: Admit your mistakes. Follow the Golden Rule. Work hard and you will be rewarded. Respect your elders. Be kind. Do the job right. Don't cheat. If you hurt someone, apologize. Share. It pays to be honest. The American Dream is attainable for everyone.

This was our truth.

But I worry about my grandchildren's and great-grandchildren's generations. They have every reason to question the old adages. Pop culture delivers the message that getting ahead and work are unrelated. It is possible to be famous for being famous. Corporations let them know that the big guys always win. Parents can work hard for decades and then be dropped with no severance, while the CEO takes home multi-million-dollar bonuses. It is hard to climb the ladder when the rungs are missing. It is easy to believe that the key to success is ruthless selfishness.

When people believe that the deck is irredeemably stacked, they lose hope. When you decide that the rule is every man for himself, you stop caring. You lose community. You undermine your family. And you are angry.

We Democrats believe in giving everyone a fair shake. We cannot—must not—let this become the America of tomorrow. It is a betrayal of our very legacy.

ENERGY AND THE ENVIRONMENT

In April of 1977, during my final term as a U.S. senator, Democratic president Jimmy Carter gave a fireside chat from the White House library, one of several sobering nationally televised speeches that he made to increase our commitment to protecting the environment and our energy resources. Carter, a plainspoken man, began this particular address: "Tonight I want to have an unpleasant talk with you about a problem unprecedented in our history."

If we don't begin to conserve now, he said, "we will feel mounting pressure to plunder the environment. We will have a crash program to build more nuclear plants, strip-mine and burn more coal, and drill more offshore wells."

Carter's strongest line, which he delivered with his fist in the air, was: "This difficult effort will be the 'moral equivalent of war.'"

Critics thought the president was showboating that night, because he wore a cardigan instead of a suit jacket. I thought the sweater was a fine touch. He was, in effect, telling the American people that if their house was chilly, they should just put on another layer instead of turning up the thermostat.

In both this speech and in his July 1979 "Crisis of Confidence" address (delivered, by the way, in a coat and tie), Carter laid out the policies the United States should take to move toward energy independence, thereby diminishing the need for U.S. involvement in the ever-turbulent Middle East. He suggested that we make practical changes: insulating homes and office buildings, driving smaller cars, carpooling, and taking public transportation.

Having just established the U.S. Department of Energy as a Cabinet-level post, Carter requested massive funds to invest in the development of alternative sources of fuel. He called for a reduction in gasoline consumption and asked Congress for the authority to impose mandatory rationing. He set import quotas. He proposed selling energy bonds. And he put solar panels on the roof of the White House.

The president's call for conservation seemed radical to many Americans, who, though worried about rising gas prices and long lines at the pumps, resisted sacrifice and change on the scale he urged.

But had we listened to Jimmy Carter then, our nation would be stronger and safer today. Instead, in the three-plus decades since he introduced the "unpleasant" topic, our energy situation has followed the dire trajectory he predicted. We have shed blood in two devastating foreign wars over oil. Gasoline has become so costly that, for many Americans, getting to work is now a substantial expense. Offshore drilling poses the risk of dramatic blowouts like the 2010 BP Horizon disaster in the Gulf of Mexico, which spilled 200 million gallons of oil. And strip-mining has been joined by mountaintop removal, an even more ravaging process, as we feed our endless need for reliable energy. And of course we are dependent on these energy sources until we create viable alternatives to take the pressure off.

Today, as a people we are still addicted to oil, overheated winters and cold summers, instant gratification over caring for our environment. We suffer from what President Barack Obama calls "amnesia": "We cannot keep going from shock to trance on the issue of energy security, rushing to propose action when gas prices rise, then hitting the snooze button when they fall again," he said. But even as the price temporarily fluctuates, in the long term it will undoubtedly rise, spurred by demand from China and India, whose 2.5 billion citizens aspire to the same comforts and conveniences we enjoy.

With 313 million people, the United States represents 4.5 percent of the world population—and we're the consumers of 25 percent of the world's oil. Out of every five barrels we use, one comes from a country our own State Department classifies as dangerous or unstable. Our oil habit has forced us to betray our own democratic principles, turning us into hypocrites and alienating moderates in the Middle East.

Consider this: in 1922, when I was born, the total U.S. population was 110 million people—roughly a third of what it is now. While I don't know what percentage of the world's goods we consumed nearly nine decades ago, I do know this: household workhorses like the washing machine and dryer had only recently come on the market, and a refrigerator cost more than a Model T. My family and I considered these items to be marvelous luxuries. Today, new houses come with three-car garages. And besides a TV in every room, we've got our computer, iPad, cell phone, iPod nano, and Wii, all of which share one thing: they ultimately depend on electricity. We plug them in without thinking—and likely, without knowing—where the electrical current comes from.

It's heartening to feel we live in the land of plenty. But as Democrats—and Americans—we are obliged to lead our country in a direction that is both sustainable and moral, even when there are short-term costs, such as those foreseen by Jimmy Carter. Stewardship of the environment, including decreasing carbon emissions, reducing our consumption of oil, and weaning ourselves from our dependence on foreign resources, should be among our most urgent national—and national security—priorities. Lawmakers must do what is good for their constituents even if they wind up paying at the ballot box. Do not be confused: "Drill, baby, drill!" is a slogan, not an energy policy.

How can we move past the one-step-forward, two-steps-back political dance that Washington has perfected? In his 1980 campaign, Ronald Reagan promised to abolish the 55-mile-per-hour speed limit, a conservation measure imposed after the 1973 Arab oil embargo. And one of his first acts as president was to order the removal of the solar panels Jimmy Carter had installed on the White House roof.

I've always been sorry that, in the days after 9/11, President Bush did not call for modernizing fuel efficiency standards (as President Obama is now)—a move that would have significantly reduced both our oil use and the amount of money we spend on oil from some of the very countries conspiring to destroy us. National security was paramount on our minds. American unity and the can-do spirit were higher than they had been since the Second World War. We were ready for large-scale sacrifice. We craved a way to heal. This was the time to make a case against using foreign oil. This was the time to allocate federal funds for the research and development of new technology. This was the time to start the construction of a national system of bullet trains just as during World War II citizens in my hometown and across the country bought bonds, planted victory gardens, ate less butter and meat, and saved foil and scrap metal for the war effort. President Bush didn't really tell us to shop: that's a myth. But the opportunity for the public to undertake meaningful change was missed all the same. Time passed. Partisan politics returned. In 2003, Congress passed a tax bill as part of President Bush's economic stimulus plan that offered a $100,000 tax credit to business owners who bought a vehicle that weighed at least 6,000 pounds fully loaded, including SUVs and Hummers. Contrast that to the puny $2,000 tax credit Congress gave to those who bought fuel-efficient hybrid cars, an extension of a decade-old law passed to encourage consumers to buy electric cars.

Energy and environmental issues should not belong to Democrats or Republicans. But while the nation has procrastinated in addressing these problems, the phenomenon that former vice president Al Gore termed "an inconvenient truth" has already begun to affect us.

In fact, global warming is not just inconvenient. It can be deadly. Hurricanes. The flooding of the mighty Mississippi River. Record drought in Texas. With 2010 being the warmest year in recorded history, the extreme weather made it seem like we were living in biblical times.

I have endured epic weather before, and I would not wish it on anyone. Growing up in South Dakota during the Depression, I remember watching farmers shielding their eyes from the sun, waiting for rain that didn't come, and watching our topsoil whipped in the air in choking dust storms that made the daytime sky seem like a moonless night. The Dust Bowl was caused by a combination of drought and poor farming practices. We learned that lesson, but, in the second half of the twentieth century, failed to take to heart others about our climate. In 2010, when the National Academy of Sciences issued "the most comprehensive report ever on climate change," Pamela Matson, Stanford University's dean of the School of Earth Sciences, who chaired one of five panels organized by the academy at Congress's request, made what is happening chillingly clear: "Climate change is occurring, the Earth is warming," she said. "Concentrations of carbon dioxide are increasing, and there are very clear fingerprints that link [those effects] to humans." This stark pronouncement was bolstered by a 2010 National Academy of Sciences survey of 1,372 scientists, 97 percent of whom agreed that it is "very likely" mankind is responsible for "most of the unequivocal warming of the Earth's average global temperature."

Some conservatives say that we are simply experiencing a cyclical weather pattern, not a chronic manmade problem. I have seen such skepticism before, and it was proved wrong. Remember those experts who said smoking didn't cause cancer?

We are bickering amongst ourselves while Rome burns, or in this case floods. Let's stop making change around the edges—or, worse, doing the exact opposite of what is called for. In Europe, most countries have invested in carbon-reduction technology and use a combination of loans, tax breaks, and regulations to cap or trade emissions. Just as FDR built the Tennessee Valley Authority in 1933 to generate electricity and development, we need the full force of the federal government behind us to diversify beyond the old and not-so-old standbys of oil, natural gas, diesel, and nuclear fuels—and even beyond corn ethanol. (While it is a so-called biofuel, ethanol is one that takes away from a necessary food source, but other advanced biofuels made from low-input crops, such as agricultural waste, switchgrass, or algae, hold the potential to replace millions of gallons of gasoline without threatening our food supply.) Hybrid cars are one alternative, and we need to develop others, including plug-in hybrids and fully electric cars that can run on batteries and be recharged, with sufficient places to do so when we're away from home.

In my home state of South Dakota, I'm used to driving past field upon field of soybeans and corn, but there's every reason why our farmers should sow wind too, to sell to the energy grid as a second source of income. I'd also like to see the country embrace more solar options to help lessen our dependence on fossil-fuel-generated electricity.

Technology is not the barrier. These and other renewables are available now. But we're stuck—and we're not just falling behind, we're squandering opportunities to create jobs, generate income, and preserve our cherished planet for the future. We don't want to switch our energy dependence from one region of the world to another, but if we don't jump into the renewable energy market, we will be forced to buy solar panels, wind turbines, and advanced batteries from China and Germany.

In 2009, a federal renewable electricity standard passed the House of Representatives but failed to pass in the Democratic-led Senate due to Republican opposition. States have taken the lead in using clean, renewable power—thirty states so far have some form of renewable electricity standard. California has been the most aggressive, mandating that one-third of its energy come from solar power, windmills, and other sources of renewable energy by 2020. But a nationwide effort would go further in creating demand and encouraging private investment.

I urge our national lawmakers to stop stalling and move ahead. Instead of being thwarted by the obstacles, we need to seize the opportunities before us. I am not an alarmist, but I truly believe that if we wait too long, we will be too late. There will not be another opportunity to say we gave our best effort to fight this cause. We must do it for our children and for theirs, just as a century ago Teddy Roosevelt created a national park system entrusted with preserving America's natural resources and scenery "for the enjoyment of future generations."

Years ago when my late wife, Eleanor, and I were rearing our young family, we loved to go camping in the Great Smoky Mountains of Tennessee and North

Carolina. And in Montana, where I spend time each summer, we boast two of America's most exquisite national parks: Glacier National Park and Yellowstone National Park. These beautiful sites truly are refuges. I'd hate to think what these places would look like now if they had been left to the laissez-faire approach of a less progressive president. (Even so, the famous glaciers of Glacier National Park are shrinking rapidly because of global warming.)

But preserving our environment and making the country energy efficient need not be—nor should be—left only to Washington's power brokers. The good news is that most of us now accept what we couldn't fathom when Jimmy Carter was president. We as individuals can make personal changes and make a real difference. The conscientious among us carry reusable bags to the grocery store. We recycle now. We don't litter anymore. Probably to anyone under thirty that sounds like a no-brainer, but I remember that before Lady Bird Johnson's campaign to beautify America's highways, we were in the habit of chucking out trash as we drove along—our gum wrappers tossed right out of the car window as we flew down the interstates.

We can all do more—citizens, government, business. We do not have to stay quiet. A patriot, or a Democrat—words I use interchangeably—can and should criticize the government when we see that it's on the wrong track. Just as the Vietnam War protests changed the course of our nation, leadership—and a new sense of purpose and direction—can come from the ground up. It is invigorating to remember that we the people can also make a difference on national security issues, climate change, and the economy. This is part of who we are as a nation.

In 1962 it was a Democrat, John F. Kennedy, who said, "We choose to go to the moon in this decade and do the other things, not because they are easy, but because they are hard, because that goal will serve to organize and measure the best of our energies and skills, because that challenge is one that we are willing to accept, one we are unwilling to postpone, and which we intend to win."

A half century later, it is time for us to challenge

ourselves to do something that will require equal tenacity: take care of the world we live in.

We Democrats will surely have to take the lead. There was a time when support for public health, clean energy, and the environment had bipartisan support. But nowadays many GOP officials and nearly all of the Republican presidential candidates deny the relationship between carbon dioxide pollution and climate change. They're against providing seed money to invest in the clean energy technology of the future while they support billions of dollars in annual tax breaks for big oil. Where Republicans are the party with a stubborn disregard for the facts before them, viewing the world as they wish it were instead of how it really is, Democrats have the courage to accept the truth, to embrace change, to look toward the future. And while remembering the experiences of the past, it is toward the future that we must look.

THE MIDDLE EAST

In March 1975 I flew 5,912 miles to have lunch with Golda Meir, the prime minister of Israel. When I got there she canceled.

The reason? As chairman of the U.S. Senate Foreign Relations Subcommittee on Near Eastern and South and Central Asian Affairs, I stopped off in Beruit and met with the exiled Yasser Arafat, chairman of the Palestine Liberation Organization.

My tour, which also included stopovers in Egypt and Saudi Arabia, came during a tumultuous time in the region. In 1973, Arab countries attacked Israel on Yom Kippur, the holiest day of the Jewish calendar. Six years earlier, in 1967, the Voice of the Arabs radio station promised "extermination of Zionist existence." Instead, Israel fended off Arab armies in the Six-Day War, a victory that turned the Jewish state into an occupying nation. Both sides were, and remain, steeped in bitterness, anger, and hate. Mrs. Meir once pronounced: "There is no such thing as a Palestinian people . . . they didn't exist."

I knew going in that the chance I could help forge peace between Israel and the Palestinians was admittedly reed slim. But I felt I had to try.

When Mrs. Meir read in the newspaper that I had talked with Arafat, she refused to meet with me and turned me over to the Israeli defense minister, Shimon Peres. Peres understood that I didn't seek out Arafat because I agreed with everything he said. I went to see him because a reed-slim chance is better than no chance at all. Meeting with only one side would guarantee increased animosity. I listened to Peres and came away with a lifelong friend.

As Democrats we know the value of listening to all points of view. This is the only way to forge peace among nations.

I have long believed that if we Americans are to be honest brokers in the Arab-Israeli peace process, we have to conduct ourselves in an evenhanded way. This has not been an easy posture for us to sustain, especially for us Democrats. American Jewish voters usually favor the Democratic Party. They tend to be liberal, humane, informed people. I recall their strong backing of me in the presidential race of 1972 as well as in my long Senate career.

Understandably, the American Jewish community is more sympathetic to Israel than to the Palestinians and the Arab states. But if we Americans are to be successful peace brokers, we have to be as sensitive toward Arab concerns and aspirations as we are to the Israelis'.

The formula for a just and lasting peace settlement has been clear ever since the United Nations overwhelmingly approved U.N. Security Council Resolution 242 following the 1967 War. The land Israeli forces seized must be returned to the Palestinians as Resolution 242 provided. Violating the U.N. formula, the Israelis have built a number of homes on land long held by the Palestinians and precious to them. Mrs. Meir once described the illegal housing settlements as "facts on the ground."

The problem with this assumption is that these "facts" are on Palestinian ground. That land should have been returned to the Palestinians in 1967. Until that is done, I see no peace between Israel and the Palestinians.

I do not believe we Democrats are helping either the Israelis or the Palestinians when we simply go along with an Israeli position that cannot possibly lead to peace. We need to make clear to the Israelis and their friends in the United States that we admire Israel and want them to have the blessings of peace and prosperity. The Israeli government should halt these settlements today and then work out a plan to assist the existing settlers in locating elsewhere in Israel.

An American Democrat is first and foremost an American patriot. This calls us to place the well-being of America as our highest loyalty. I believe it is in the best interest of America for us to be equally fair to the Israelis and the Arabs. That is also the role for an effective and honest Middle East peace broker. The Bible tells us that the Israelis are God's chosen people. That being the case, the Israelis must not ignore the biblical injunction: "What does it profit a man if he gain the whole world and loses his own soul?"

What does it profit the Israelis if they cling to the Palestinian land and gain the hatred and violence of the Palestinians and the Arab world?

"If the Palestinians do not achieve stability," Arafat told me during my 1975 visit, "the area will not achieve stability."

Many years later, Arafat entered negotiations with one of Mrs. Meir's successors, Yitzhak Rabin. I was at the White House in 1993 when President Bill Clinton brought the two former adversaries together for that famously moving handshake on the South Lawn. Just two years after that—because of his efforts to make peace—Rabin was assassinated by a right-wing Israeli. To my mind, it was probably the most costly assassination of the twentieth century. Arafat died in 2004. And more than thirty-five years after my trip, neither the Palestinians nor the region has achieved stability.

Nevertheless, dramatic changes have been taking place in the Middle East. I was captivated by the "Arab Spring" of 2011, when ordinary people in a number of countries gathered in the streets to protest the dictators who for decades had kept their own citizens down. Autocrats in Tunisia and Egypt were forced from office, while those in Bahrain and Syria at this writing were holding on by might. An uprising against Libya's strongman, Colonel Muammar el-Qaddafi, led to a violent civil war, and another in Yemen was threatening, at the time of this writing, to do the same.

And, of course, the United States finally killed Osama bin Laden.

Like so many Americans, I applaud people in the Middle East and North Africa who want to have a say in how their nations are governed. And, like so many people around the world, I do not mourn the death of a terrorist responsible for murdering thousands. But there is much more that needs to be done to bring stability to this volatile part of the world.

Besides facilitating a peace agreement between Israel and the Palestinians, we must bring home our troops from Iraq and Afghanistan. When I met with President Obama at the White House in March 2011, I begged him to withdraw from Afghanistan immediately—and completely. The president countered by saying that the best advice he had received, notably from the military experts, was to take a middle course, meaning a gradual drawdown. "Mr. President," I said, "there is a reason the American people elected you and not David Petraeus to be commander in chief."

Let's first look at Iraq. Barack Obama opposed the Iraq war from the outset, speaking against it as an Illinois state senator. In 2004 he ran for the U.S. Senate as an antiwar candidate, lambasting President George W. Bush for invading the country on what turned out to be false pretenses. Later, he introduced a Senate bill calling on President Bush to withdraw

American combat brigades from Iraq by the end of March 2008. When he was running for the Democratic presidential nomination, Obama distinguished himself from his closest competitors by pointing out that he had opposed the war from the beginning and that they were late converts to the cause.

Once he got to the White House, President Obama did the right thing by declaring a formal end to combat and by drawing down American troops. Now he has to finish the job—by the end of 2011, as promised. As I write, some 46,000 American troops remain in Iraq. They have become victims of vicious rocket attacks, the targets of hard-liners aiming to take credit for pushing the occupiers out. Despite the danger to American troops, the outrageous cost of the war, and its needlessness, some people—including our conservative Republican Speaker of the House, John A. Boehner—believe that keeping soldiers there is critical to our immediate and long-term national security interests.

He couldn't be more wrong. Iraq never was critical to our national security, and it surely isn't now.

There were no weapons of mass destruction, as President Bush asserted in his breathless march to war, and that country had nothing to do with the terrorist attacks of 2001. If we didn't know that then (and I would argue that we had a pretty good inkling), we certainly do now. Every day we spend in Iraq is costly on so many levels. To quote now-senator John Kerry's 1971 congressional testimony against the Vietnam War, I wouldn't want to have to be the one to explain to grieving parents why their child "was the last man to die for a mistake."

There was no valid reason for President Bush to order an American invasion of Iraq. It was a violation of international law that claimed thousands of lives and cost us $3 trillion—nearly a fourth of our national debt. Our war in Afghanistan will doubtless constitute another one-fourth of our national debt. While the killing and crippling of our soldiers is the chief cost of war, it is no small matter that half of our national debt is the result of two wars we never should have launched.

It is time for Iraqis to take responsibility for their

own country. When George W. Bush first ran for president in 2000, he said he was against the idea of nation building. Once elected, it was an entirely different story. He seemed to want to turn every country, but especially Iraq, into a miniature America. I'm as much of a small-*D* democrat as the next American. But we can't foist our way of doing things on the rest of the world. We have to let people in other countries decide for themselves what kind of government works best for them.

The same holds true for Afghanistan. We invaded Afghanistan in the fall of 2001 with one goal in mind: to root out terrorism. We wanted to stop the ruling Taliban from giving safe haven to bin Laden and his al-Qaeda killers. So we bombed it back several centuries and changed the government. But then what?

We stayed. And we're still there. Although President Obama announced his decision to withdraw 10,000 troops in 2011 and 23,000 more in 2012, my timetable there is different. To me, the answer is clear: Bring our soldiers home. Now. A decade is long enough.

There are all kinds of reasons people cite for why we should keep troops in Afghanistan. But if I may be candid, none of them makes a lick of sense.

First, they say we need to keep troops in the Middle East to combat terrorism, particularly al-Qaeda. That's a fear tactic. President Bush and his vice president, Dick Cheney, used it unapologetically and to great effect for years. Even after they botched the chance to kill or capture bin Laden early in the war in Afghanistan and embroidered lies to start a war with Iraq, they managed to scare Americans into giving them an undeserved second term.

To be clear, I'm not downplaying the tragedies wrought by terrorists and the toll that the threat of terrorism takes on our people. Certainly, we need to take precautions to protect our nation and the people who dwell in it. That we have done and continue to do. We have built up the best army, the best navy, the best marine corps and air force in history. We're perfectly capable of defending our shores.

By keeping bases in the Middle East—even in countries whose rulers welcome us, like Bahrain—we do not squelch terror. Instead, we perpetuate it by sowing anger among people who are already enraged by the regrettable conditions in which they live. Perhaps no country illustrates this better than Pakistan, the very place where we tracked down and killed bin Laden. Even as we argue that we are making their part of the world safer, Pakistanis, by and large, loathe the United States. Although the United States has given their country $20 billion in aid over a decade, Pakistanis view us not as their protector nor as their friend but as their invader, as their enemy. By continuing to bomb the border region that Pakistan shares with Afghanistan, we are creating a new generation of terrorists, plain and simple.

Another argument frequently raised for keeping our troops in Afghanistan is the protection of human rights. People who put forth this argument contend that we need to stay in Afghanistan to prevent an erosion of the humanitarian gains and civil rights that have taken hold since we drove the Taliban from power in late 2001. In particular, they say, we must protect Afghan women and girls. This is a laudable goal, one that Democrats might be expected to embrace. After all, our party has been at the forefront of the battle for women's rights in this country, so why not around the globe? Aren't we the party that supports equal pay, family and medical leave, and abortion rights? Haven't we backed the Violence Against Women Act and opposed countless forms of discrimination?

We, as Democrats and as Americans, undoubtedly want for women around the world what we want for women at home. But that doesn't mean we are in a position to deliver it.

It is true that in the fifteen years in which the Taliban were in charge, women and girls in Afghanistan had virtually no rights. They were prohibited from working outside the home, from venturing into public without a male relative, even from seeking medical help from a male doctor. Abuse was widespread: women accused of adultery were stoned to death, women who allowed a glimpse of skin were whipped. We all have seen photographs of Afghan women clad from head to shoes in blue burkas, which forces them to view the world through small mesh rectangles and makes them practically invisible in their own land.

After the United States invaded Afghanistan in 2001, the world took notice of the plight of Afghan women. First Lady Laura Bush spoke out on their behalf. Governments and nonprofits took up the cause. Things started to change.

Imagine: only 5,000 Afghan girls attended school in 2001. Now Oxfam reports that 2.4 million do. Women have paying jobs, they appear on TV, they even serve in Parliament.

Admittedly, the gains are neither complete nor universal. Afghan women have a long way to go to achieve the kind of basic human rights that all people deserve. However, that is not an argument for keeping our troops in their cities and towns, not a reason to continue risking American lives. Mark my words: when we finally withdraw, whether it's tomorrow or ten years from now, the gains that have been made on behalf of Afghans in general and women in particular will be reversed. We can't keep troops around the world to make everyone behave as we would like.

Generally, I'm an optimist. But it would take more than that to think things are going to get better there. I remember reading Paul Theroux's *The Great Railway Bazaar* some years ago. When he went to Afghanistan, he wrote that there was no excuse for that country. It's not really a country as you and I understand it. It's a collection of tribes, many of which despise each other. They have resisted occupation going back to Alexander the Great in 334 B.C. No other country has ever been able to work its will there. The Soviets invaded Afghanistan in 1979, were mired in a war there for a decade, and finally left in humiliation. (Afghanistan is widely considered the "Soviet Vietnam.") Meanwhile, millions of Afghans were displaced, and many of them fled to Pakistan or Iran. More than a million Afghans were killed, as were nearly 15,000 Soviet soldiers. Many more on both sides were permanently disabled or disfigured by bullets, bombs, or land mines. It was a colossal mess.

I don't think we'll succeed any more than the Soviets did.

No matter how long we stay in Afghanistan, the Taliban will stay longer. Sure, we'll kill some of them, maybe even a lot of them. But for what? To be honest, I'm not even sure how we would know if we won. Would we count up the number of Taliban dead and compare it to the number of American dead? Would we remake the economy so that it's no longer dependent on the heroin trade? Would we wait until women had equal rights (a long wait, for sure)? What is the definition of "victory"?

One lesson we definitely learned from President Bush is how *not* to prosecute war—or peace. The Bush Doctrine—which I define as the willingness to act unilaterally and preventively—dramatically changed the primary tenets of America's foreign policy. Principles of deterrence and containment that had been followed by Democratic and Republican presidents, including President George H. W. Bush, for decades were abandoned. Do you realize that George W. Bush is the first United States president to actually *start* a war overseas? By contrast, when his father sent American troops to the Persian Gulf in 1991, it was in response to Iraq's invasion of Kuwait and with the backing of a broad coalition of nations that his administration took the time to bring together.

Luckily, President Obama seems to have learned from some of the mistakes of his predecessor. When Colonel Muammar el-Qaddafi started massacring rebels in Libya, the president didn't rush in as if America were the sole savior of all oppressed people. Instead, he worked closely with NATO to institute a no-fly zone and try to prevent further killings. On the occasions that we have to use force—and I believe we should do so sparingly—this is the way to go about it. So I was appalled by the House Republicans' hypocrisy in refusing to give our commander in chief the vote to continue the mission. Can you imagine how loudly the Republicans would have cried foul if we Democrats had done the same?

If we really want to bring stability to that most unstable region of the world, we should bank less on the military and more on diplomacy, development, and support for new, democratic institutions. It is by fostering friendships and alliances, not by flexing our military muscle, that we can best ensure that al-Qaeda and other terrorist organizations do not gain (or regain) a foothold in countries that are experiencing transformation.

Which brings me back to the Israelis and Palestinians. We must encourage peace between these two peoples in order to stabilize the region. Not only is this the right course of action on moral grounds—Palestinians deserve their own state and Israelis deserve to live without existential threats—it is a way to reduce tensions in the entire Middle East. For years, terrorists throughout the region have used Israel as a scapegoat for their own murderous behavior and as a rallying cry against Israel's patron, the United States. "The lack of progress toward Middle East peace clearly is an issue that is exploited by our adversaries in the region, and a source of political challenges," said then–Secretary of Defense Robert Gates in March 2010, which is why "the U.S. has considered peace in the Middle East to be a national security interest for decades."

If Israel no longer occupies Palestinian territories—if the two peoples can live side by side peacefully—we can remove that excuse and further isolate terrorist organizations such as al-Qaeda, Hezbollah, and Hamas.

I agreed with President Obama when he laid out his view of where negotiations between these long-standing adversaries should begin (or, more accurately, begin again, following a hiatus). In a speech that was risky for a president facing a reelection campaign, he articulated what had long been a behind-the-scenes consensus: the starting point for peace talks should be pre-1967 borders with mutually agreed-upon land swaps. In other words, the Palestinians would get back most of the land that Israel occupied following the Six-Day War; Israel would retain some of the more significant settlements it has erected in the West Bank in exchange for other land along the border.

This is a sound and rational position, one that would require each side to give up something in the quest for peace. It is a position I have been advocating since those days in the 1970s when Mrs. Meir canceled our lunch.

Sadly, the president's speech was seized on by Israeli prime minister Benjamin Netanyahu and American Republican leaders, who tried to use it to their political advantage. Both the prime minister and the Republicans criticized President Obama, saying that he jeopardized Israel's security and pushed an ally "under the bus." This is not so. What the president was attempting was to clear the way for a peace agreement that would allow Israelis to live free from the fear of suicide bombers and war, and that would permit Palestinians to finally have a state of their own.

It was the right thing to do.

Israel's continued occupation of the West Bank and the Gaza Strip is bad not only for the Palestinians, who lack some of the basic freedoms we in America hold so dear, but for Israel itself. It will not be long before the Palestinians' higher birth rate makes them a majority population in the land. At that point, Israel will have to reassess its claim that it is really a representative democracy—or abandon its identity as a Jewish state.

Negotiating peace with the Palestinians, and ending its occupation of their lands, is the only way for Israel to secure its own future, to shed the yoke of an occupier, and to give its children and the Palestinian children the peace they deserve.

President Obama showed courage when he gave his speech, and I admire him for it. He did not hold his finger up to see which way the political winds were blowing any more than Harry S. Truman did in 1948 when he backed the birth of the Israeli state. Democrats, some of whom immediately sought to distance themselves from President Obama on this issue, must instead stand with him and give him the political backing he needs to press the Israeli government to accept this starting point. Jewish Democrats, in particular, must demonstrate that they support a so-called two-state solution (which polls show the majority of Jews in America and Israel do) and that they will not abandon the party for prodding Israel to move toward that goal. We must not allow Republicans to turn this into a wedge issue. Peace is far too important to be reduced to that.

UNIVERSAL
HEALTH CARE

My mother grew up in Calgary, Alberta, and many of my relatives and their families still live there. My Canadian cousins are amazed that, as advanced as we are in some ways, the United States still doesn't have universal health care. I'm with them. The logic for instituting it here is so flawless, it hardly bears discussion.

The Canadian approach makes sense to me, particularly since American health statistics are not in our favor. During their lifetime, one in nine women in the United States will get breast cancer. Each year, one in eight babies—about 500,000—will be born prematurely, and around 700,000 people will have a stroke. And at any one time four to five million people have dementia. Countless people will struggle with addiction or clinical depression or both.

It's a given that there will come a time when you or a family member will need extensive care. For our family, it was when my late wife, Eleanor, developed heart problems, and when our beloved daughter Terry battled alcohol addiction. After many years and many attempts at long-term sobriety, Terry died, and I fell headlong into a deep depression that was resolved when I was treated at the Johns Hopkins Hospital in Baltimore.

Even during those grim times, I knew how fortunate we were to have health insurance. In 2009, at the height of the recent recession, I ached for the one-sixth of the U.S. population—nearly 51 million people—who were without it. A few days in the hospital would be financially catastrophic for them. With luck and care they might recover from a serious illness, but their solvency would not.

Serious illness can wipe out a middle-class family.

Researchers from Harvard Law School, Harvard Medical School, and Ohio University found that most personal bankruptcies are filed by people whose medical bills are more than 10 percent of their income. And about 75 percent of them had medical insurance but were felled by co-pays and uncovered costs. Some of my American relatives are among the even larger group of people who, because of medical debt, neared bankruptcy without going over the edge.

The inability to fix someone you love, the back-and-forth bounce between hope and despair, the week-in, week-out care, is exhausting emotionally and physically. I have visited with a great many people who have reached the far end of their tether, pulled between their job and the hospital, mortgage payments and hospital bills.

In medicine, the good news can also be bad: the more medical advances, the more wonder drugs there are, and the better-trained our physicians, the higher the costs. I think that's a burden we ought to spread over the whole society.

In 2010, Barack Obama and the Democrats in Congress did an outstanding job in passing the Patient Protection and Affordable Care Act to make health insurance available for every American. The bill passed without a single Republican vote.

The law is being phased in over five years, but it has already eliminated some of the major shortcomings of the private insurance system. It has made health coverage available to more children and young adults, ended lifetime limits on coverage, made more preventive services available at no cost, improved pharmaceutical coverage for seniors on Medicare, and provided tax credits to small businesses that insure their employees. The law also prohibits insurers from the heinous practice of denying coverage to children who have preexisting conditions, a provision that later will be extended to adults. It offers much-needed discipline to the insurance companies, which have called the shots for far too long.

But I think we should go further.

We should replace the 906-page bill, which I'm

sure many lawmakers and most citizens haven't read, with a seven-word sentence that reads: "Congress hereby extends Medicare to all Americans."

My firsthand experience with Medicare has convinced me that a Medicare-like plan, or single-payer system such as Canada enjoys, should apply to everyone, not just to old duffers like me. Such universal coverage would mean that anyone, of any age, could go to a doctor of their choice—and the government would pay the bill. It would help young families raising children and lift the burden from hiring older workers, who, according to the Congressional Research Service, are unemployed at higher rates and for longer periods than their under-fifty-five counterparts, in part because their health insurance costs more.

We need more preventive care and more clinics to manage routine and chronic illnesses, vaccinations, and prenatal care so that fewer people end up in the emergency room. We need more screenings. One reason health insurance is so expensive is that without regular screenings, diseases are not discovered until they have progressed. Simply put, stage one cancer is easier and cheaper to eradicate than stage two, three, and four.

The idea of universal coverage has been around since Franklin Roosevelt's day, when Frances Perkins, FDR's secretary of labor and the first woman to hold a Cabinet post, put it on the table. The mother of Social Security, Perkins understood that Americans needed a health safety net. In 1945, only seven months into his presidency, Harry Truman tried in vain to sell the idea of a national health insurance plan to Congress. And we all remember that the health care debate in Congress was not the Clintons' most successful hour. So here we are—still without national health care.

But Republicans already think we've gone too far. Conservatives and the medical lobby have worked hard to spread rumors and horror stories about universal care. They don't bother to make a distinction between socialized medicine—the system in place in the UK, the U.S. military, and the U.S. Department of Veterans Affairs—in which the government runs the hospitals and pays doctors' salaries—and a single-payer system, in which doctors in private practice are paid a fee-for-service from government funds.

We've all heard the GOP's arguments: You'll get bottom-rung doctors from offshore medical schools. Your doctor will have no time to talk with you. You'll never get the same doctor twice. You'll wait for hours. They'll skimp on tests and treatments.

This is all nonsense.

Along with Social Security, Medicare is the federal government's most successful and perhaps most popular program. Since it was signed into law by Lyndon Johnson in 1965, it has provided medical care to all Americans sixty-five and older. The program is beloved for one reason: it is extremely effective. I get to go to the doctors and specialists I choose. Republicans often suggest that Medicare is government intrusion. Well, I have never heard a single recipient complain that Medicare is bureaucratic meddling.

During the health care debate of 2010, Republicans carried on like Chicken Little, not only scaring citizens into believing that the Patient Protection and

Affordable Care Act would doom them to substandard care but, along the way, would break the budget. Soon after the bill passed, twelve state attorneys general, all Republicans, filed lawsuits seeking to declare the mandate to buy insurance illegal. If they win, the bill will be overturned. A majority of voters were made nervous enough to help the GOP take control of the House and gain seats in the Senate in 2010. As soon as Republicans took over the House of Representatives in January 2011, they voted to repeal the ten-month-old law. Of course, this was an empty political gesture; they knew the Democratic majority in the Senate would never abandon the measure.

Now conservatives are taking an "If it ain't broke, break it" approach. The Republican message is that Medicare is going to go bankrupt, and the party leadership has proposed privatizing the system. Were this to go through, the nonpartisan Congressional Budget Office estimates it would force individual seniors to pay more than $12,510 for medical care each year—twice as much as they would pay under Medicare—starting in 2022.

I feel so strongly about universal health coverage that I think a person who doesn't favor it would probably be more at home in the Republican Party. Good health care is so essential that I'd argue that the federal government that defends us against enemies abroad should also protect us from illness at home.

ALCOHOL AND
DRUG ADDICTION

L osing a national presidential election, as I did to Richard Nixon in 1972, is a sad experience. But it is a skinned elbow next to the irreparable pain of losing a child. Our Teresa Jane McGovern, called Terry from the day she was born in 1949, was the middle of our five children. She died in Madison, Wisconsin, in 1994. She froze to death, falling down in a snow-covered parking lot while intoxicated. She was an alcoholic.

Our family is close: we cherish each other. We not only treasured Terry, we had the financial resources to pay for her prodigious and repeated efforts to get—and stay—sober. We cheered her, helped her enter rehab, attended family meetings, and finally, in hopes of helping her to confront her alcohol dependence, distanced ourselves. We even agreed to have her committed to a long-term care facility if it became the only way to save her.

Many alcoholics have no such underpinnings. And sometimes all the support in the world isn't enough. The disease is often stronger than love. It was stronger than Terry's deep desire to get well.

Alcoholism cuts across every demographic. It affects the young and the old, the poor and the rich, the meek and the mighty. It strikes more men than women, more African Americans than whites. As I wrote in my 1996 book, *Terry: My Daughter's Life-and-Death Struggle with Alcoholism*, this disease "is like a thief in the night. It can steal up on you and seize your life, liberty, and pursuit of happiness before you comprehend what happened."

There are far too many stolen lives. In the United States alone, there are 17.6 million people who abuse alcohol—meaning their drinking is destructive *and* addictive. They are alcoholics. What does that mean?

It means that they are so hooked on alcohol that they can't quit the excessive intake even when they desperately want to stop drinking. Many drinkers start young—1.6 percent of twelve- to thirteen-year-olds are binge drinkers (five drinks for males or four drinks for females within about two hours); 7 percent of fourteen- to fifteen-year-olds; 17 percent of sixteen- to seventeen-year-olds, and nearly 35 percent of eighteen- to twenty-year-olds—before they reach the legal drinking age, according to the 2009 National Survey on Drug Use and Health. Starting young could be a predictor of future alcohol abuse. I know it was for Terry, who took her first drink—a Colt 45—when she was just thirteen.

As a society, we tend to see addictions as weaknesses that could be overcome. Perhaps that is a way of assuring ourselves that it can't happen to us. But it can. And it does.

Addiction is an illness like diabetes, multiple sclerosis, or cancer. And like them, genetics plays a part. Some 75,000 Americans die from an alcohol-related disease or accident every year. There are about 38,000

drug deaths each year, with painkillers like Oxy-
Contin, morphine, and methadone accounting for
more deaths than cocaine and heroin combined. And
every person who dies was once somebody's lovable
little girl or boy—like Terry.

America needs to treat addiction like the illness
it is. We can start by putting more money toward research. We need to find out how to help people like
Terry, who suffered from chronic relapses. In the years
since she died, scientists have developed medications,
including naltrexone, intended to curb cravings by
blocking the brain receptors that make drinking plea-
surable.

The late Betty Ford's public admission that she
was addicted to alcohol and painkillers showed unprecedented courage in 1980. She lent her name to the
now well-known California clinic to embolden other
people to take on their addictions. And First Lady
Rosalynn Carter shone the nation's attention on mental illness: Terry was among the 50 percent of alcoholics who also suffer depression. Mrs. Carter lobbied
for the passage of a 2007 law forcing insurance com-

panies to cover treatment just as they do for physical illnesses. Barack Obama's 2010 Patient Protection and Affordable Care Act extends coverage for mental health and substance abuse.

As Democrats, we need to heighten attention to alcoholism, its ripple effects on families, and, ultimately, on our country—divorce, domestic abuse, and absenteeism from work and school. Taking this complex issue head-on would make for a more productive nation. And while there's a debate on the effects of advertising on children's behavior, I can't help but think that some, if not a considerable portion, of the $4.5 billion a year spent on alcoholic beverage marketing falls on eyes and ears made all the more vulnerable because they are young. As with tobacco advertising, I believe our children would be better off without Madison Avenue giving them the impression that drinking is cool. Moderate drinking can be enjoyable for most of us, but not for alcoholics.

We also need to remember that although alcohol is legal, it is still a drug. Certainly, a major difference is that while we tolerate alcoholism, often our response to drug addiction is to punish the addicts. American prisons are filled with people whose crime was that they used illegal drugs or sold small amounts of them in order to support their habits.

Terry nearly went to prison once.

It was July 1968, and I was in Los Angeles to speak at a luncheon in tribute to Robert Kennedy. We had been close friends, and I had spoken to Bobby by telephone only a few minutes before he was shot on June 4. My noontime address paid homage to his legacy: "We can yet serve the end he so tenderly sought for us all—'to tame the savageness of man, and make gentle the life of the world.'" As I prepared to deliver it, I picked up the *Los Angeles Times* and was greeted with this front-page headline: "Senator's Daughter Arrested on Drug Charge," news that Eleanor had delivered to me by telephone the previous night.

On summer vacation from Dakota Wesleyan University, Terry had been arrested in Rapid City, South Dakota, where she had been working on behalf of my Senate reelection campaign. She had been staying in a Black Hills motel with other student campaign workers. An employee thought she smelled marijuana. Knowing that my daughter was probably among the campaigners on hand, the woman—a staunch Republican—called the local GOP chairman. He called the Republican attorney general, who contacted the Rapid City police. The police obtained a search warrant and, at midnight, knocked on the door of the room Terry was sharing with a friend. There they found a small container of pot.

It was a trifling amount. But legally it was a big deal. South Dakota had just enacted a law setting a mandatory prison sentence of at least five years for anyone convicted of possessing marijuana for a first offense. Terry and her roommate were the first two people charged under the new law. We hired some top-notch lawyers, who discovered a technicality that invalidated the search, and the judge dismissed the case.

This kind of thinking—arrest the problem by arresting the offenders—was boosted by Richard Nixon's "War on Drugs," a response to the growing heroin epidemic among U.S. soldiers in Vietnam in 1971. In the forty years since, we have arrested 40 million people on drug charges and spent $1 trillion. It has not worked.

In a letter to Congress in 1977, Jimmy Carter, noting that "stringent laws" to discourage marijuana use since it was declared illegal in 1937 had been unsuccessful, recommended that we decriminalize possession of up to one ounce. "Penalties against possession of a drug should not be more damaging to an individual than the use of the drug itself," he wrote.

But Ronald Reagan, who was elected after Carter's single term, escalated the fight. He signed a drug bill in 1986 that included money to build new prisons and created stringent federal mandatory drug sentencing. Between 1981, when he took office, and 2009, the U.S. prison population jumped from 550,000 to 2.3 million people. In that same period, drug-related prisoners increased 1,100 percent. With 794 people out of every 100,000 behind bars, the United States has more people in jail than thirty-six European countries combined. So it's no wonder the American Civil Liberties Union calls us the "world's largest incarcerator."

Here's what I think: dealers—those who provide or sell drugs to children—and users who commit violent crimes certainly must be punished. But many of the people filling our state and county lockups—and there are well over a million—are small-time users and addicts who might be productive citizens if they can gain control over their disease.

Democrats are often viewed as being "soft" on crime. This is a ridiculous charge that angers me every bit as much as the insinuation that we are somehow less patriotic than Republicans. During Bill Clinton's administration, violent crime, which peaked in 1992, dropped for eight consecutive years. It's now lower than it has been in four decades. As with our defense budget, the amount of money we spend each year on keeping people in jail could be put to better use. California has spent more on prisons than on education, and the conditions are terribly overcrowded, so much so that in 2011 the U.S. Supreme Court ruled the situation a human rights violation.

The Obama administration has taken a step in the right direction by promoting the use of drug courts, which allow judges to order offenders into treatment programs as an alternative to prison. Government and private studies have shown not only that drug courts help offenders control their addictions but that, by doing so, they reduce the crime rate. Addicts don't commit crimes because they are criminals; they resort to crime because they need money to feed their craving. If they can regain control over their lives and stay sober or drug-free, they no longer need to steal in order to buy their drug of choice.

In 2011 the Global Commission on Drug Policy, which included former presidents and prime ministers, business and government leaders, human rights activists and writers, left no room for ambiguity on this question. "The global war on drugs has failed," it said. The report shows that between 1998 and 2008, the use of opiates leapt 34.5 percent, cocaine 27 percent, and cannabis 8.5 percent. Instead of acting as a deterrent, our nation's tough-on-drugs approach backfired spectacularly. The report recommended that we treat users who do no harm to others as patients and not as criminals, substituting treatment for jail time. It also suggested that governments experiment with legalizing some drugs, particularly marijuana, and to concentrate efforts on violent criminal organizations, not on low-level producers and dealers. It highlighted several European countries that can provide an effective model for us to follow.

Some states are starting to make positive changes on their own. Faced with overcrowded prisons and outrageous corrections costs, they are reducing sentences for low-risk, nonviolent drug users and creating treatment programs intended to help them stay out of prison for good and become productive members of society. More states—and the federal government—need to follow suit.

When we do send drug offenders to prison, we need to provide them with treatment and reentry programs that will help them reintegrate into their communities. Every year we release almost 750,000 drug offenders from prison. Many of them don't stay out for long, in part because we don't do enough to help them transition to new and better lives.

Democrats, it is time that we made drug and

alcohol treatment a priority. Republicans often lay claim to the family values mantle, but if ever there was an issue that affects families, it is this. Addiction touches—or frightens—every one of us. And while we're at it, we need to put "Just Say No" to rest. I consider Nancy Reagan a friend, one who has many admirable qualities. But children who have addictive tendencies can't live by just saying no. We need to give our children workable strategies for dealing with the drugs—both legal and illegal—that will confront them. If saying no worked, my dear daughter would not have died.

CONCLUSION:

HONING THE DEMOCRATIC MESSAGE

Democrats, if ever there was a moment to define ourselves boldly, to stick to our ideals, it is now. I was inspired to enter politics by Adlai Stevenson's eloquent late-night acceptance speech at the 1952 Democratic National Convention in Chicago. I was at home in Mitchell, South Dakota, up on a ladder, painting our living room, the radio turned low so as not to wake my family. Stevenson, who was running against the popular war hero Dwight D. Eisenhower, had little chance of winning. But I found his message so moving that I put down my paintbrush, climbed off the ladder, and sank back into an old chair to listen.

His concern, he said, "is not just winning this election but how it is won . . . I hope and pray that we Democrats, win or lose, can campaign not as a crusade to exterminate the opposing Party, as our opponents seem to prefer, but as a great opportunity to educate and elevate a people . . ."

By the time Stevenson finished, I was ready to sign on to his campaign. Lacking money and political connections, I decided to write a series of op-ed pieces for the *Mitchell Daily Republic* on the historical issues that separated Republicans and Democrats. They were a hit. Not long after, the Democratic Party state chairman asked me to leave my teaching job and create a new one: executive secretary for the Democratic state party. And the rest, as we former professors like to say, is history.

Democrats and Republicans want the same for our nation: a healthy economy, well-educated children, enough jobs to go around, a safe and vibrant society. Democrats are the party of Andrew Jackson, Woodrow Wilson, and Franklin Roosevelt. Republicans are the party of Abraham Lincoln, Theodore Roosevelt, and Dwight D. Eisenhower. Our nation has achieved its greatness through the leadership of each.

But we have different ideas about how to get there—and that is as it should be. This is how democracy works. Our founding fathers understood that the push and pull of debate clarifies issues and refines solutions. They assumed that ultimately the people steering our government would put aside self-interest to achieve the common good.

When I was in the Senate, from 1963 to 1981, it was a congenial place, despite the fact that I disagreed sharply with Republicans on many issues. One example of compromise: Mark Hatfield, the Oregon Republican, and I cosponsored a controversial amendment to end the Vietnam War. There are countless more.

Such compromise does not—and has not—always come easily. In 1856, during the lead-up to the Civil War, Representative Preston Brooks, a South Carolina Democrat, entered the Senate and struck Massachusetts senator Charles Sumner repeatedly over the head with a cane—almost killing him—for remarks Sumner had made against Brooks's cousin. Fortunately our differences are rarely so dramatic. Still, there are plenty of colorful stories of political adversaries brandishing (and sometimes firing) pistols and throwing punches on the congressional floor and off.

Once in a while I almost think that old-fashioned fisticuffs seem preferable to the insidious atmosphere that now prevails in Washington. At least it was straightforward. Best, of course, is to fight hard for party principles and negotiate a deal. But while President Obama promised to govern in a spirit of bipartisanship, that, by definition, involves two sides, and today's Republican Party, with its zealous Tea Party wing, appears unwilling to give any ground.

Even before the Tea Party became a force, however, politics as usual had turned mean-spirited. I'm afraid that what Adlai Stevenson said nearly six decades ago about the GOP wanting to "exterminate the opposing party" at any cost is truer than ever.

But there is far too much at stake to waste a moment hand-wringing or complaining. Right now we have 14 million men and women without jobs, millions of families in bankruptcy and foreclosure, and some 50 million people without health insurance. We have families who cannot afford to send their children to preschool and others fretting over how to pay for college. We have Americans who go without enough to eat and others for whom nutritious food is simply not within reach. We have men and women in prison for drug use who should instead be in treatment. We have soldiers fighting in distant wars who should be at home with their families. We have immigrants who have traveled under horrific conditions in search of a better life that still eludes them in our midst. Never in modern times have so many people needed a hand so desperately.

These are our pressing concerns, not the petty politics of our opposition. One topic that may divide

Democrats and place some of us outside the president's view are the two seemingly endless and mistaken wars in Iraq and Afghanistan. In my view, we never should have invaded either of these countries.

Yes, Republicans have worked to tear America apart by creating wedge issues and by falsely characterizing Democratic positions. Yes, Republicans have commandeered God, family, and flag—things we all value, no matter what our party affiliations or how flush our bank accounts. Yes, Republicans have taken the offensive on such highly personal matters as abortion, an area that should not even be involved in politics. (It is essentially a women's issue, since none of us men can ever be pregnant or have an abortion. The woman will make the decision after consultation with her partner, her doctor, and her spiritual adviser. Several years ago, when Eleanor and I were in Minneapolis, we watched a televised debate that included the wrestler Jesse Ventura, who was running for governor. When they asked all three candidates where they stood on abortion, Jesse said: "I don't know anything about abortion. I'd just leave it to the women."

Jesse unexpectedly won the election. I thought his answer was on the money.)

Demagoguery on these topics makes us angry—and it should.

But what matters most at this critical juncture, as the future of our nation is hammered out in the halls of Congress, is that we Democrats remember who we are: we are the party of solutions. We are, as I emphasized, the party of the New Deal, the New Frontier, the Great Society, and the War on Poverty.

We are the party that believes we can't let the strong kick aside the weak. Our party believes that poor children should be as well educated as those from wealthy families. We believe that everyone should pay their fair share of taxes and that everyone should have access to health care.

Let me reiterate: almost every great federal program put in place since World War II was conceived by Democrats. Among them: Medicare, Medicaid, Social Security, the Food Stamp Program, the Voting Rights Act, Head Start, the Peace Corps, the National School Lunch Program, Lilly Ledbetter Fair

Pay Act, collective bargaining laws, the Fair Labor Standards Act, the State Children's Health Insurance Program, the Family and Medical Leave Act, and the Patient Protection and Affordable Care Act.

I can think of no federal initiative now celebrated by both Democrats and Republicans that began as a conservative program launched over Democratic opposition. If there is one tucked away in the congressional annals, I am counting on readers to let me know.

Days before the 1936 election, as my political hero Franklin Roosevelt campaigned for his second term, he gave a famous speech in New York's Madison Square Garden in which he took stock of his many accomplishments, of how far the nation had come in securing stability, and of the Republican record of inactivity he had overcome. But he delivered his hardest punch on his opposition: "Never before in all our history have these forces been so united against one candidate as they stand today. They are unanimous in their hate for me—and I welcome their hatred."

FDR did not shrink away from his political enemies. He hit them head-on. But what consumed him
was not retaliation; it was pursuing the proactive
agenda he forged to turn our ailing nation around.

Democrats, now is our time to do the same. We
must uphold the faith of the millions of Americans
who believe in the power of government.

There are those who say that the Democrats have
failed to communicate our message effectively. I feel
strongly that the best way to correct this is to high-
light the unstoppable momentum we have created to
raise people up; the same momentum that has made
our nation a global showplace.

But it's true that for all the GOP's negative chatter
about the liberal media, Democrats don't have the
equivalent of a Rush Limbaugh, a Sean Hannity, or a
Glenn Beck. More entertainers than journalists, the
ultraconservative media inflame national audiences
with half-truths and divisive messages. Nor do we
have one conductor such as Karl Rove who calls all of
us to sing the same verses.

This can be frustrating. When conservatives attack, we need to call them on their tactics and refute their deceptive claims on the spot. Waiting doesn't work in these days of instant news. I'm proud that we are the big-tent party, that we speak with many voices and not just with one. But we cannot let this get in the way of defending ourselves. The hours spent meeting and mulling is the same time that fabricated stories gain traction. We must react before falsehoods become "fact" on the Internet.

Still, we should never lower ourselves to spreading rumors. I'm gratified that our party, for the most part, errs on the side of fairness. We owe it to the people who elect us—and equally to those who don't—to make the best laws we can to serve the public. Our credibility means too much to risk for short-term gain.

The GOP may well be the better-oiled machine. And they know that the quickest way to win is not by campaigning on their plans for the country but by harping on how the Democrats will raise and then squander taxes.

It is unethical to use fear to win an election. And

I think the negativity that fear breeds has lasting effects on our country. Barack Obama (and Bill Clinton before him) instinctively understands how imperative it is to project optimism, to talk about our aspirations rather than our doubts, to instill hope. True leaders know that it is only by aspiring to a positive vision of our great country that we can raise her to a higher plane. America yearns for pragmatism, for leadership that can bring our country together, not divide us. The ultimate goal, as Adlai Stevenson said, is to "elevate people."

In this, we can take solace in how aggressive the Republican presidential field has so far been in their attacks against our president. Making oneself look good by making others look bad is a tactic that voters can see through.

Admittedly, these are difficult times. Our economy may be slowly recovering from a shattering recession, but it doesn't feel that way to most people. And as we struggle personally, we are also dogged by the notion that other countries are overtaking our long-held position of preeminence in the world.

Democrats, it's our job, just as it was FDR's, to restore faith in ourselves and in one another. We cannot give up hope on America now.

In June 1993, to the surprise of many of my colleagues, I went to Pat Nixon's funeral. I always thought that Mrs. Nixon had maintained her dignity through tough times, and I knew firsthand how wives get pushed out of the spotlight and elbowed by the press. I wanted to honor her memory. So I caught a ride on the plane that ferried several senators to California from Washington.

At the ceremony, held in the beautiful amphitheater of the Richard Nixon Presidential Library & Museum in Yorba Linda, President Nixon was bathed in tears. Later, when he thanked everyone for coming, he singled me out. But a reporter approached and asked me why I would come pay my respects to an old political enemy.

My answer? "You can't keep campaigning forever."

Democrats, we are the party that rises above. This is not the time to hide in the shadows or to surrender.

CONCLUSION

This is the time to step out and to step up. This is the time for us to heal our nation's rifts and to deliver on her promise as we see it: a republic that is good to all. It is not for nothing that I will go to my grave believing that ours is the greatest country on earth.

ACKNOWLEDGMENTS

This book is the brainchild of a superior editor and publisher who has been my treasured friend for many years, David Rosenthal.

I could not have completed this book in the timeline set by the publisher without the splendid assistance of Linda Kulman. She made certain that both research and composition were excellent.

GEORGE McGOVERN

.   .   .

It was an honor and pleasure to collaborate with George McGovern.

The country is better for John Podesta's founding of the Center for American Progress, and so is this book. Winnie Stachelberg generously opened up CAP to us for research on numerous fronts. I'd like to thank fellows Matthew Duss, for his help on the Middle East; Lawrence Korb, for sharing his knowledge on defense spending; Ruy Teixeira, on American politics; and Daniel Weiss, for his expertise on energy policy. Robert Greenstein and Richard Kogan at the Center on Budget and Policy Priorities provided invaluable assistance on government spending, and Marshall Matz shared his extensive knowledge of Senator McGovern's career-long work on hunger. Tom Daschle and Jeff Smith also provided wise insights.

I would like to thank Jodi Enda for her contribution and partnership. Michaela Balderston was an intelligent and energetic research assistant.

My mother, Margie Kulman, and my sisters, Betsy Kulman and Cindy Brown, gave me unbounded support. David Fauvre, Rafael Heller, Joni Walser, Nancy Zuckerbrod, and my Eastham cheering squad showed the generosity of spirit that makes them so dear to me. Katy Kelly transcended the ordinary claims of friendship, as she has done with each of my projects. Finally, I was lucky enough to come home to Ralph, Sam, and Julia each night. You are my North Star.

LINDA KULMAN